THE GREATEST
LOVE STORY
NEVER TOLD

Liberating Jesus and Mary from Christianity

Avi Raa

ALSO BY AVI

The Silent Path

In Search of I

The Ocean in a Drop

The Whirling Dervish

Where the Hell Are You Going?

Acknowledgement

The whole universe has to come together to move a single blade of grass. This book would not have been possible without the support of everything that has ever happened. I am especially grateful to my students, who record, transcribe, edit, and publish my talks.

CONTENTS

The Greatest Love Story Never Told

FOREWORD

"The Greatest Love Story Never Told" should be a mainstay in any Christian collection not because it explores the usual contentions of Christian history; but because it defies many of these traditional perceptions.

Its controversial message won't be for every Christian - but it should be, because within its challenge of Church doctrine and the extreme efforts made over history to rewrite the image of Jesus the man lies an intention to place Jesus in the kind of perspective that makes him even more of a spiritual figurehead: "When it comes to understanding Jesus, the single most important question we have failed to ask is, "What did this young man find within him that he was willing to sacrifice everything for the sake of sharing it?" If only we had asked this one question, without burdening it with a two-thousand-year-old borrowed biblical answer that he was a "Messenger of God", we would have discovered an entirely different Jesus - one more alive and vibrant than he who hung on the cross."

Vibrant, uplifting, and filled with reworkings of traditional Christian history, The Greatest Love Story Never Told indeed walks the dangerous path of revisionary works in challenging some of the most closely-held legends of Christian belief.

From Mary Magdalene's real role as the wife of Jesus and one of his apostles to her very human broken-heartedness over his crucifixion and the roots of why he was envisioned as rising from death after three days, The Greatest Love Story Never Told not only adopts a broader perspective in re-interpreting the life of Jesus, but does so with fiery passion.

Many of these passages will offer much food for thought in other ways, envisioning possibilities that could have stemmed from events if they were interpreted and presented differently: "...there is no Christianity without Mary and her internalization of Jesus' truth. If Mary Magdalene had been a man, in all likelihood her Christianity would have replaced that of Jesus'."

By now, it should be evident that, inherent in the controversial reworking of Christian history, there is enlightenment in the discovery of a living man who was something even more intriguing than the mystical figure the Church created from his life.

Christian collections willing to consider this book's revolutionary and outspoken revisionist approach to Christian history will find it sparks not only debate and food for thought, but a different, more revealing appreciation for the path Jesus walked.

Libraries appealing to Christian readers and thinkers will find *The Greatest Love Story Never Told* essential for reading groups interested in different views of how Christian fact and fancy evolved. The book encourages reflection and debate as it forms an unusual perspective on Jesus' life and the way it was taken over and interpreted by the special interests of a Church undertaking to cement its power in the world.

Diane Donavan, Senior Editor
Midwest Book Review

The Greatest Love Story Never Told

FROM THE AUTHOR:

Growing up in a typical middle-class Indian family with traditional Hindu beliefs, Jesus was never a significant part of my life, except for two occasions. One of them was during Christmas when my grandmother used to take me to the church. I was not particularly interested in the church itself, but the bustling markets that were set up outside it were fascinating to me. The sights, sounds, and smells were all strange and otherworldly, and it was a memorable experience. The other occasion was when I used to visit my girlfriend. There was a nearby church a few miles away from where I lived, and it was one of the quietest places in the city. Most Indians didn't know what to do in a church, but I knew exactly what I was doing - visiting my girlfriend.

The church was where I was first introduced to the idea of love, although not in the way one would expect. I attended a Christian school where my principal and most of my teachers had intriguing names that combined both Hindu and Christian influences. It wasn't until later that I found out that most of them were converted Christians. However, at the time, I didn't even realize I was studying in a Christian school with basic Christian discipline and principles. As a result, growing up, I didn't know much about Jesus, except that he was a figure hanging on the cross who didn't seem to mind watching love bloom between two young Hindu souls, even in such an uncomfortable position.

Years went by before I revisited the subject of Jesus. My life took me on a wildly different journey, from college and science to a career in finance, and eventually to a life of meditation. It was during this time that I was first introduced to Jesus as a mystical teacher. This was the proper introduction, not the distant "Son of God" hung on a cross, with whom I couldn't connect. Instead, I saw Jesus as a human teacher, full of wisdom, light, and insight. His story had always fascinated me, particularly the mysteries about his human life that resurfaced now and again, constantly shifting my understanding of him. Only after I had gone deep into the world of meditation and became a teacher myself did I come back to Jesus, prompted by my students' desire to understand his teachings.

Initially, this book was intended to be a spiritual discussion of the mystical teachings of Jesus as recorded in the Gnostic Gospel of Thomas. I knew that my interpretation of his teachings would differ significantly from the Bible, but I felt that a mystical perspective was the only way to fully understand his teachings. At that point, I had no doubt in my mind that Jesus was a real man and a teacher. It wasn't until I began compiling the talks for publication that I stumbled upon an entirely different story of Jesus - one that I had never anticipated. As I explored his life, from his formative years as a student in the Qumran caves and his time studying under the Nazarenes, to his conversations with his disciples, his crucifixion, and his eventual status as the world's most famous man, I began to realize that the true story of Jesus has been largely hidden from the world. The version of his story that we have been told for so long is just one interpretation, put forth by a particular group of believers that happened to become the most widespread.

As I delved deeper into the life of Jesus, I stumbled upon a name that would shake the very foundation of my understanding of Christianity - Mary Magdalene. She was not just a footnote in the story of Jesus, but rather an integral part that bound everything together. In fact, I soon realized that Mary Magdalene was as important, if not more, than Jesus himself. She held the key to some of the biggest secrets of his life, and her story completely transformed my understanding of Jesus and his message.

The book began to take on a life of its own. It no longer wanted to be limited to merely interpreting some of Jesus' verses; instead, it sought to uncover the greatest hidden truths of his life. As the book progressed, it started to read more like a mystery novel than a simple spiritual discourse. I found myself nearly powerless to control the narrative; it was as though the story had a life of its own and was using me to tell itself. Even the title just dropped from nowhere; one of my students read the manuscript and exclaimed, "This is the greatest love story I've ever read." Thus, the name of the book.

I came to realize that understanding the true love story of Jesus and Mary Magdalene is impossible without delving into the Church's efforts to conceal their story. Thus, a significant portion of the book is dedicated to dispelling misconceptions about who Jesus was. However, I am aware that my findings may challenge the beliefs of some traditional Christians and Jews, and may even hurt their sentiments. Since I am not a practicing Christian, I did not have to constantly worry about offending traditional Christian beliefs. I approached the story with an open mind, allowing it to guide me. Every time I was faced with a decision between not offending Christian beliefs and staying true to the story, I chose to remain true to the story. This book was a labor of love, inspired by my passion for Jesus and Mary Magdalene, and for the billions of believers who long to connect with their story. If I inadvertently hurt anyone's sentiments, I would like to apologize and state that it was not my intention.

As I put the final words on the page, I couldn't help but feel that I wasn't writing the book. I was merely a vessel. Truth had totally used me in its service. I was as much a spectator watching this book unfold as you will be when you read it. In a way we would pretty much be going through the same emotions of shock, disbelief, anger, fear, pain, joy and enlightenment, in discovering the story of Jesus and Mary Magdalene, two extraordinary individuals whose love for each other transcends everything we are familiar with. Let us begin and see where the story takes us.

The Greatest Love Story Never Told

DREAMS & NIGHTMARES

By the dawn of the first century, the Romans had occupied Jerusalem and were ruling it under a puppet king, Herod. This was a precarious time for the Jews, who were fighting a losing battle, defending their holy land against an alien race that differed from them in every way imaginable. Into this seething cauldron of conflicting cultures walks a young Jew by the name of Jesus, bringing his radical spiritual message of freedom and transcendence. He could not have chosen a more inappropriate place or time to do this.

In his youthful innocence and unrestrained enthusiasm, Jesus had failed to consider the possibility that in Jerusalem's hostile environment of suspicion and mistrust, everything he says can be mis-understood. Pointing to that undivided spiritual realm he had discovered within him, and using a simple allegorical language familiar to the Jews, he preaches, "Return, the kingdom of heaven is within you."

The Jewish mind, clouded in fear, misses the subtlety of his message entirely and hears only the words

"Kingdom" and "Heaven." Within a week of arriving in Jerusalem, the body of this young man, once full of life and light, was hanging on a Roman cross bearing the inscription, "Jesus the Nazarene - King of the Jews."

Although our image of Jesus is inseparable from that of a man nailed to a crossbeam of wood, crucifixion wasn't a special punishment specifically awarded to Jesus. As far as the Romans were concerned, there was nothing special about him - he was just another rebellious Jew who had to be reminded of his place in the newly established social order of Jerusalem.

Romans crucified Jews all the time, even at the slightest hint of a rebellion - sometimes to punish, but mostly to send a message. Contrary to the popular image of three crosses on the hill of Golgotha, Roman crosses lined the busy streets of Jerusalem by the hundreds. Pinned to them were low-hanging Jewish bodies left at the mercy of dogs and vultures.

Being fully aware of the Jewish sentiments for the dead and how much they abhorred the hellish idea of a human body being devoured by wild beasts, the Romans ensured that decomposing corpses stayed on the cross for as long as possible, as passing Jews squirmed to avoid their twisted shadows.

Crucifixion wasn't just a punishment - it was an exhibition of Roman brutality; a statement of authority unleashed at the first sign of unrest. If one has to pick an image from the past to accurately represent the dark ages of man - his fears and insecurities, ignorance and brutality - none would be more befitting than the Roman cross. Yet, such a cross, capable of representing only the basest of human emotions - hate, agony, and death - is ironically, also the world's most revered religious symbol.

The Roman cross, more than any other symbol, stands to testify to the fact that religious rituals and traditions emerge, not around truth, but around dead and decaying symbolisms, professing to fill that void in Man's consciousness; his age-old quest for certainty.

Although the nascent Christian movement began as an independent spiritual quest revolving around the mystical teachings of Jesus, it soon stagnated into a belief system obsessed with symbols of Jesus' death - the cross, crucifixion, and the whole drama surrounding it. Over time, the binding ideologies of the Church became a self-fulfilling prophecy, systematically eliminating any evidence pointing to the ordinary human story of Jesus, almost entirely replacing his life with his death.

Little did Jesus know that the very same ignorance he was rebelling against would one day make a mockery of his truth, tear into its living flesh, and turn the memory of its grisly execution into the world's most celebrated religious symbol - all in the name of love.

Much of what we now recognize as Christianity was born in 325 AD, almost three hundred years after Jesus' crucifixion, at an ecumenical council convened by the Roman Emperor Constantine. More than three hundred Christian bishops from the eastern half of the Roman Empire had gathered for their first council at Nicaea - a small town nestled between the Black Sea and the Mediterranean. They were summoned to settle their theological differences and agree upon a single Christian doctrine, to further Constantine's political ambitions of unifying his kingdom under one God.

Like ravenous wolves scavenging a carcass, these holy men debated and argued over every aspect of Jesus' image, picking and choosing from the collection of gospels that lay in front of them, guided by one all-important question: "Who was Jesus?"

Of the hundreds of gospels, including some written by Jesus' own disciples, only a handful of distorted texts serving Roman interests made the cut to become the Bible as we know it today. The debate of Jesus' divinity was settled once and for all using man's oldest political whip - the last refuge of ignorance - consensual voting.

Armed with a book to control the illiterate masses and a sword to assure its unconditional acceptance, the Roman Empire was all set to unleash its new phase of politics: to rule by the will of God. The mission of this two-faced religio-political campaign was nothing short of ridding the world of every other existing and fledgling expression of Truth, to replace it all with its one God-ordained religion: Christendom.

To this end, the Church diligently went about its business of erasing the first three hundred years of Christian history by destroying or converting nascent Christian churches, and burning all heretical scriptures that refused to fit inside its narrow theological cage.

Backed by a mighty empire, this once-persecuted fringe religious movement began to spread like wildfire, engulfing everything in its path, to eventually become the world's largest religion. The same revolutionary words of Jesus, meant to awaken the human spirit from its deep social and religious stupor, in the hands of an ambitious, religio-political organization, became the perfect tool for subjugation, snatching away from the individual the very freedom it was meant to usher in.

The oppressive reign of the Church would continue uninterrupted for nearly a millennium, dragging Western civilization further along its dark and bloody trail. The first meaningful resistance to the authority of the Church - its scandalous double life, greed, and corruption, would emerge in the fifteenth century, when a German theologian, challenging the Catholic doctrine, nails his thesis of dissent to a church door, igniting a new Christian movement.

Martin Luther was the first to translate and publish the Bible in a language other than Latin, effectively marking the beginning of the end of a thousand-year monopoly of the Church in the business of printing and distributing the Bible. The Protestant Reformation which began as a movement against the suffocating dogmatic rule of the Church, would eventually branch off into more than thirty thousand independent Jesus denominations, each interpreting the Bible in its own unique way.

While the Protestants managed to escape the institution of Catholic Christianity, they could not break away from the Bible that was forged by the very sword of the Roman Emperor Constantine. Eventually, Christianity would become a confusing sect of independent ideologies, all carved out of the same Bible stories that had mutilated, beyond recognition, the simple life and message of a human teacher.

The historical Jesus and the Jesus of the Bible are two entirely different creatures. While one is a fully flesh and blood human teacher - a Jewish rabbi crucified for questioning the rigid orthodox beliefs of his faith, the other is a religious messiah - the "Son of God," sacrificed for the sins of humanity, who alone is the key to man's salvation.

If the real Jesus is an ordinary man who depended on the love and care of his disciples to his delicate feet, which were often chapped from long barefoot walks, the biblical Jesus is a super-human, capable of performing all kinds of miracles, including walking on water, raising the dead, and ascending to heaven.

While Jesus, the man, lived and died striving to awaken individuals from their deep slumber of superstition and ignorance, urging them to return to their internal realm of peace and certainty he called the "kingdom of heaven", the divine Jesus is sitting high up in the sky, in heaven, on an unreachable pedestal, secretly conspiring with priests and popes, helping them live like kings here on earth.

ROOTS & BRANCHES

The word "Bible" is now so unconditionally Christian that many have altogether forgotten that the original Hebrew Bible has a history of more than three thousand years, going all the way back to the time of Moses. From Latin "biblia", literally meaning "books", the original Jewish Bible refers to a collection of five books - Genesis, Exodus, Leviticus, Numbers, and Deuteronomy, along with poems and other Hebrew writings, altogether representing hundreds of years of the Jewish storytelling tradition, all recorded long before the time of Jesus.

In fact, the Christian Bible is simply referred to as a New Testament of the original Hebrew Bible. While this biblical nomenclature may seem logical and fitting, what's confounding is the obviousness with which it is acknowledging Christianity's true origins. Unlike other monotheistic religions, Christianity was never meant to be a new religion dedicated solely to the remembrance of the life and message of one man around whom it was supposed to revolve. Christianity, at its core, is still a religion true in every detail to its

Jewish imagination, on whose foundations it was originally built.

Except for the introduction of Jesus into its scriptures as a new messiah, the ancient Jewish religion has continued uninterrupted in its rituals and traditions for well over three millennia. It is not by some divine intervention that the Jewish festival of lights, "Hanukkah," celebrated every year during late November and December, coincides with "Christmas," the Christian holiday celebrating Jesus' birth. Baptism, the indispensable rite of passage to becoming a Christian, proclaimed to be the only gateway to Jesus' "Kingdom of Heaven," is essentially a Jewish practice: The "Son of God" himself had to be baptized as a part of his initiation into a Jewish mystical order.

The ritual of circumcision, which Jesus himself was clearly against, is another example of a Jewish practice that has lived on in Christianity. When asked about the religious significance of circumcision, Jesus trashes the practice, saying, "If God intended circumcision for his children, they would have taken birth already circumcised." One has to wonder then, how can Christianity be regarded as a religion dedicated solely to the life and message of Jesus, while it continues to cling to an archaic Jewish tradition Jesus himself was vehemently against.

Used in its original spiritual sense, the word "circumcision," literally meaning "cutting around," was intended to help break away from unnecessary external distractions and indulgences to make way for a quieter inner life. Over time, as has been the case with many spiritual practices, the idea deteriorated into a literal, physical ritual of cutting the foreskin around the penis - a morbid and twisted inter-pretation of "abstaining from sex." Fortunately, however, this horrendous practice did not extend to women, who were considered unworthy of pursuing a higher spiritual way of life.

The most important question that needs to be answered is not why Christianity has chosen to embrace this ghastly Jewish practice, but instead, how did Jesus get mixed up in this strange assortment of severed Jewish beliefs we now recognize as Christianity?

In 70 AD, the Romans had destroyed the temple in Jerusalem and were threatening to displace the Jews from their homeland. On the verge of losing its tradition, culture, and identity, the Jewish religion was forced to appeal to the sentiments of the non-Jewish gentile population in order to survive.

In the melting pot of Jerusalem's religious tensions, conflicts, and politics, the life and teachings of an enlightened Jesus got intermixed with the Jewish religion, to eventually become Christianity. The very same Jews, who were persecuting Christians for their weird practices, began accepting Jesus into their scriptures to gain acceptance among the rapidly expanding gentile population of Jerusalem. If not for this alteration, it is quite possible that by now Judaism would be an extinct religion. By accepting Jesus into its long messianic tradition, the struggling Jewish religion began to thrive, to see its highest point with Constantine's full endorsement.

Right under the nose of Roman persecution, archaic Jewish beliefs and practices quietly slipped into the clothes of Christianity to gain Roman acceptance and eventually become the world's largest faith. The face of Christianity might be that of Jesus, but its beating heart is very much Jewish. One only has to scratch the surface of Christianity to see how alive and kicking ancient Judaism still is.

The New Testament Bible is not attempting to tell the story of Jesus, but rather its own story using the popular image of Jesus, who was brought inside the Jewish scriptures to reaffirm ancient Judaism's prophetic history. This is why Bible stories bear no resemblance to Jesus' actual life. The biblical Jesus, instead of challenging outdated Jewish ideologies, is in full support of them. Matthew offers a genealogy of Jesus drawing from the lineage of David, which is an absolute necessity if Jesus is to be recognized as a Jewish messiah. Jesus' mother, father, and grand-mother are also archetypical Jews who fit into their assigned roles perfectly. One sect of Judaism accepted Jesus into its messianic tradition but not before washing him clean, giving him a new haircut, and teaching him some Jewish manners.

Jesus' sharp revolutionary words questioning the orthodox Jewish belief system were altered to reaffirm Judaism's dogmatic practices. His revo-lutionary teachings, meant to shake the human race out of its social, political, and religious slumber, were converted to easy-to-digest bedtime stories, around which people could huddle together and feel good about themselves.

Since Jesus did not have much of a family or social life, it was easy to introduce tailored Jewish characters to fill in the gaps and assist in carrying forward his Jewish lineage. In fact, the biblical Jesus is so fictitious and predictably Jewish that his entire story can be recreated by using ancient Jewish parables.

The least important character in the biblical story of Jesus is Jesus himself. Practically anyone could replace him without altering the original Jewish essence and purpose of his story. This awkward inclusion of Jesus into the Jewish scriptures has led many to question whether he was even a real person or just a figment of the Jewish imagination.

For the sake of truth and respect for Jesus, the debate regarding his divine or human nature must be resolved. While the awakened Jesus lived and died urging people to follow his example, referring to him as the only begotten "Son of God" is an insult to his unique identity, life, and message.

By denying Jesus his rightful place among the people, we have reduced a great spiritual teacher to a mute symbol of suffering. Jesus' life, his search for truth, and his struggles would lose their significance if he were not an ordinary man. His message is relevant precisely because he was a mortal human being, otherwise there would be no reason to care about this enigmatic figure.

If Jesus was not pointing to the Truth that already existed within humans, why should his life be worth remembering, and his words worth reflecting on? If Jesus was not born like the rest of us and did not struggle like the rest of us to reach his truth, then his message is utterly meaningless to us humans who are fully bound to the physical laws of life. For Jesus' life to make sense, he cannot be anything other than a fully flesh and blood human being.

By calling Jesus the only "Son of God" and making him an end unto himself, we have erected an unassailable wall between Jesus and his life. This wall, built using the ragged bricks of biblical theology and the blood, sweat, and tears of the innocent, stands firm and cold between a man and his truth.

Stuck on the other side of this wall, the common man is severed from having any meaningful human connection with Jesus. This dividing wall is the foundation of the Christian faith. Christianity's success has always depended on keeping Jesus high up on this pedestal, far away from the reach of the believers. By separating Jesus from his people, the Church has made it incredibly hard for his original teachings to take root in their hearts and minds.

By unconditionally accepting Jesus as a divine being, we have denied ourselves the opportunity to study and understand his incredible human story of truth, love, and courage. As a man and a teacher, Jesus' life could have been an inspiration for many to walk their own path to self-perfection. But, as the "Son of God" nailed to a cross, he has been nothing more than a distraction.

More than anything else, Jesus' teachings alone should testify to his human roots and upbringing. Although he was guiding people to a higher truth, his choice of words to describe that truth was extraordinarily simple, earthy, and human.

Jesus' message of a higher life doesn't drop from the heavens. Rather, it appears to have sprouted from the same desert sands that nourished his earthly body. His expressions of life are never far from the rich daily experiences of common people. He speaks not as a man who has been endowed with some special wisdom that is denied to others, but as someone who has always been one with those around him.

Just like any ordinary human being in possession of some great wisdom, Jesus struggles to communicate his message, fails more often than he succeeds, feels burdened and helpless, and often gets frustrated and angry. Everything about Jesus' manners, thoughts, and actions screams "human."

It is puzzling that a man like Jesus, who can supposedly walk on water and breathe life into the dead, doesn't use his special powers to accomplish that one thing he was apparently sent for. Throughout his teachings, there is not one instance where Jesus used his special abilities - if he had any - to influence people or help them better understand his message. When people fail to grasp what he is trying to say, he expresses his frustration in as plain a language as best he can.

In one instance he says, "I took my place in the midst of the world, and I appeared to them in flesh. I found all of them intoxicated; I found none of them thirsty. And my soul became afflicted for the sons of men because they are blind in their hearts and do not have sight; for empty they came into the world, and empty, too, they seek to leave the world."

These are not the words of a "Son of God" who is in full control of what is happening around him. Rather, they are the words of a rejected, helpless, human teacher who appears to be burdened by the sheer weight of the task he has set out to accomplish.

It is clear that Jesus had been teaching for not more than three or four years before he was crucified. All the teachings recorded by his disciples are from this brief period in time. There is no evidence to suggest that he ever taught during the first thirty years of his life. In fact, there is hardly anything recorded about Jesus' life before he began teaching. All the childhood Bible stories attributed to him were later imaginations inserted to emphasize the belief that he was born special.

This habit of glorifying a teacher's ordinary past is neither new nor unique to Christianity. The lives of Abraham, Moses, Buddha and Muhammad are filled with similar miraculous childhood stories, rooted not in factual history but in the emotions of the community believing in them.

For the first thirty years of his life, Jesus was virtually unknown. He was just an ordinary man whom nobody cared to think about or remember in any special way. The Bible narrates the birth story of Jesus, so why wasn't anyone keeping up with this divine being? With his unprecedented status and all his miraculous powers, how did this "Son of God" manage to stay hidden for most of his life? How is it even possible to miss a man like Jesus, who could supposedly turn water into wine?

The reason for the missing years of Jesus' early life isn't a mystery. Before his spiritual awakening around the age of thirty, Jesus was just another ordinary man. Like Buddha, Muhammad, and many other enlightened individuals, he acquired his unique understanding of life through a spiritual process that has remained essentially unchanged since the beginning.

An ordinary carpenter became "Christ", the awakened one, not by the intervention of God, but by pursuing higher knowledge. Jesus discovered an ancient spiritual path in the desert and had pursued it until it revealed its secrets. He transformed his ordinary human life into an expression of Truth through rigorous, dedicated spiritual effort and practice. Having realized the ultimate truth, from amidst a sea of people and depths of obscurity, he bursts into human consciousness as a fully self-realized man.

Truth has ways of impressing itself upon people, even when they seem not to recognize it. People could hardly understand Jesus, but they were still drawn to him. His words resonated within them at depths they didn't know existed. Jesus' words were so deep and insightful that they appeared to emanate from a source beyond the familiar human realm.

Ironically, this profound understanding of life is what made it possible for Jesus' teachings to be misinterpreted in so many different ways. Many groups, unable to accurately grasp the meaning of his message, began to attribute his extraordinary wisdom to an imaginary other-worldly source. Over time, these small, independent, streams of wisdom found their way to the heart of the Roman Empire, from where they were sanctified and redistributed through the official doctrine of the Christian faith, the Holy Bible.

Beyond centuries of misunderstanding and manipulation, historical evidence and scholarly interpretation, dogmatic theologies and religious beliefs, Jesus' true identity hides in his own words. Nowhere else does his individuality shine as brightly as it does in his teachings.

Even to this day, Jesus' words are relevant only because they point to a truth that can take one beyond the daily struggles of life - beyond fear and uncertainty. His original teachings, when interpreted correctly, have the power to help an individual break free from the self-imposed shackles of life.

Jesus' message is relevant because humanity is still wallowing in the same religious dogmatism and superstition he was fighting during his time. It has been more than two thousand years since Jesus lived, but very little has changed. As a species, we are still searching for answers, and we will continue to do so.

It is indeed possible to shake off centuries of religious conditioning and take a fresh look at Jesus' life and message from a new perspective, provided we are willing to consider that there are more civilized ways of connecting with a mystic like Jesus than by drinking his blood and eating his flesh.

The Greatest Love Story Never Told

THE MAN AND THE MYSTIC

Not all individuals submit their lives equally to the measuring scale of history. The brighter the shades of one's individuality, the harder it is to cage them inside the dimly lit dungeons of human understanding. It's as though, in their defiant silence, some lives are trying to tell us that they are too precious to be confined to such an ordinary thing as understanding.

Perhaps this is why it has been easier for us to grasp the intentions and motivations of a group driven by common ideologies, as opposed to comprehending the life of a free-spirited individual in pursuit of their unique destiny.

If we've had such a difficult time understanding ordinary human beings who spend most of their time semi-consciously wandering the wilderness of life in search of meaning and purpose, then how much more challenging it must be to understand the life and message of a fully conscious man like Jesus? It isn't surprising that Jesus is both the most worshiped and the least understood human being in history.

Jesus, the man, is relevant to us only because hidden somewhere in his parables are precious gems of transcendental wisdom capable of illuminating some of the deepest and darkest recesses of the human spirit. His original verses deserve a special place in human literature and consciousness primarily because they were delivered not as mindless religious sermons to tranquilize the masses, but as scientific expositions of the human condition, to help an individual descend to the depths of their inner being.

When it comes to understanding Jesus, the single most important question we have failed to ask is, "What did this young man find within himself that he was willing to sacrifice everything for the sake of sharing it?" If only we had asked this one question, without burdening it with a two-thousand-year-old borrowed biblical answer that he was a "Messenger of God," we would have discovered an entirely different Jesus - one more alive and vibrant than he who hung on the cross.

One of the most difficult things to understand about Jesus is that, unlike other historical figures, he was not a product of his social, political, or religious conditioning. What set him apart came neither from his "special" birth nor from his gruesome death. Rather, it came from that single internal experience of

Truth, without which he would have been just another Jew crucified by the Romans. This is why it is impossible to understand Jesus by analyzing his life objectively, using historical information alone. One needs a deeper, more intuitive understanding of his teachings to be able to make any sense of his life.

Trying to recreate an image of Jesus using bits and pieces of moth-eaten information from the past, while ignoring his all-important teachings, can only lead to such preposterous conclusions as, he was the "Son of God" sent to save mankind. The secret to understanding Jesus lies not in the familiar verses of the Bible but in a rarely explored spiritual dimension of his upbringing: those all-important missing years of his life.

History, at best, records only the words and actions of extraordinary individuals. It seldom captures the resilience of their rebellious spirits or the forces that helped shape them. Although the life of the biblical Jesus unfolds in the backdrop of a noisy, chaotic, religio-political environment, everything that defined Jesus, the man, came from an altogether different realm of silence and stillness that he had carefully cultivated within himself, using the ancient discipline of "Mysticism."

Hidden within every religion, lesser-known spiritual sects have always existed, dedicated to experientially solving the riddle of life. The Vedantists of Hinduism, the Sufis of Islam, and the Gnostics of Christianity, are just a few examples. While mainstream religions have mostly been preoccupied with expanding their scope and scale of operations, striving to draw as many individuals as possible into their fishing net of faith, these often-ridiculed mystical branches have quietly kept the flame of truth and transcendence burning. They guide a courageous few on the narrow path of Self-Realization. One such community of hermetic Essenes, dwelling in desert caves at the foot of Mount Carmel, was the "Nazarenes."

The word "Nazarene" comes from Aramaic "Nazorai," meaning "to watch." The Nazarenes were mystics who willingly chose to distance themselves from the noise and clutter of mainstream society to dedicate themselves to the spiritual discipline of "Watching" - a form of meditation practiced in silence, solitude, and stillness to explore the hidden mysteries of life.

The Nazarenes led simple lives, spending most of their time in meditation and study, internalizing ancient scriptures, and guiding each other along the way. Their daily practice revolved around striving to transcend the deep-rooted human condition of fear and uncertainty and move toward their simple, natural higher selves, in a process of internal cleansing they called "baptism."

Far from its biblical interpretation, the Nazarene baptism was an extraordinarily real, physical, and psychological process of self-transformation. A ritual bath in the Jordan River marked only the beginning of an initiate's long and arduous journey.

At around the age of thirteen, a young Jew named Jesus was wandering along the Jordan River when he heard, for the first time, the esoteric teachings of John the Baptist. Enchanted by the preacher's vision, he immediately decided to leave home and join the community of the Nazarenes, an extraordinary moment of decision that irreversibly altered the course of his life as well as that of human history.

For several years, Jesus diligently toiled along the spiritual path under the guidance of his teacher, studying, meditating, and serving the community. He grew by leaps and bounds in his understanding of the human phenomenon and the fabric of life supporting it. Just as Buddha had done five hundred years before him, Jesus descended to his inner world of thoughts, dreams, and desires in silence, searching for the meaning of life and the source of human suffering. Through the regular practice of "meditative watching," his perceptual clarity deepened, and his awareness expanded. Slowly, he lost his fear of people and their judgments, becoming a complete individual - a world unto himself.

In one such moment of deep meditation, Jesus breaks through the imaginary barrier between his mind and body to experience a transcendental state of reality known as "Awakening," changing everything he knew about himself and the world around him.

The young boy who had gone into those caves in search of Truth was no longer the same person returning from them. Jesus now had a realization that would set him on a path very different from others. He had not acquired any special physical powers that could alter the course of his life or foresee his impending doom. However, mentally and spiritually, he was now a fully realized man, capable of guiding individuals along the ancient path of Awakening.

Basking in the glory of his new-found realization, Jesus runs into the streets declaring, "Return; the kingdom of heaven is within you." He takes upon himself the arduous task of drawing the attention of deeply conditioned human minds toward his lofty vision of inner freedom. He was doing this, not because he was the "Son of God" or the "Chosen One," but simply because he was acting on that natural human impulse to help, compelling him to share what he regarded as "Good News."

In his innocent eagerness, however, Jesus fails to reflect on the sheer magnanimity of the task that lay ahead of him - especially considering the fact that he was now as different from his fellow Jews as any ordinary man could be. For over a decade, the company of holy men and their spiritual words of wisdom had shielded him from the chaotic marketplace of life, to which he now has to take his delicate message, hoping that it doesn't get trampled under the old worn-out boots of religious orthodoxy.

There was something about Jesus - the way he spoke, moved, and preached, that disturbed the peace of the Jews. Jesus was not a religious messiah, social reformer, or philosopher. He was a mystic who would have, no doubt, come across as an authoritative and even arrogant man, with the Truth he had realized within him being the source of his authority.

As a spiritual man who had transcended his base human desires and fears, Jesus would have spoken with a certainty that was almost disturbing. He would have had no trouble expressing his intentions clearly and powerfully. Both meekness and arrogance share their common roots in ignorance, but truth has its own unique flavor.

Somewhere between being polite and being rude, there exists honesty. When Jesus spoke, he was neither kind nor arrogant - he was simply truthful. Like a spewing volcano, he was neither considerate nor hateful, only exploding in the ecstasy of the truth he could not keep to himself.

A deeply conditioned human mind, steeped in fear and superstition, could have easily mistaken Jesus' certainty for boastful arrogance. Not surprisingly, the truth and simplicity of his words pierced the hearts of the Jews like daggers tipped with poison.

One need not speculate on the nature of Jesus' personality, as he made it abundantly clear through his words and actions that he had no ambition of gaining the love and acceptance of those he was trying to help. If he had any such intentions, he would have most certainly refrained from saying such things as, "I have cast fire upon the world, and see, I am guarding it until it blazes."

Jesus wasn't preaching to unite people toward some common cause. He was vehemently dividing them from each other so they could stand alone by the strength of their own individuality. In his characteristic, brutally honest manner, he says, "Perhaps, people think that I have come to cast peace upon the world. They do not know that I have come to cast conflicts upon the earth: fire, sword, war. For there will be five in a house: there will be three against two and two against three, father against son and son against father, and they will all stand alone."

Strange words, coming from the mouth of a sacrificial lamb sent to be slaughtered for the sins of humanity. Jesus was a rebel in every sense of the term. He spoke not to support the traditional beliefs of his people, but to awaken them from their deep slumber of life. If his words do not create tremendous disturbance, chaos, and confusion, they aren't his words.

HE WAS SERIOUS

In December 1945, two Bedouin farmers were digging for fertilizer at the base of a cliff near the Egyptian town of Nag Hammadi when they chanced upon a buried jar containing leather-bound papyrus scrolls of Coptic Gospels. Among these ancient texts, mostly written during the first few centuries of Christian history, were three of particular significance: "The Sophia of Jesus Christ," "The Gospel of Mary Magdalene," and "The Gnostic Gospel of Thomas." They contain some of the most incredible original teachings of Jesus recorded by his closest disciples.

These heretical documents, most likely buried by their owners to keep them from being destroyed, and now in the Coptic Museum in Cairo, present irrefutable evidence that Jesus was, indeed, an ordinary human teacher - perhaps even a married man and a father. After two thousand years of being hidden in the dark, these forgotten scriptures are finally seeing the light of day, revealing for the first time the conveniently hidden human story of Jesus, challenging his traditional, almost universally accepted Christian "Son of God" image.

Of all those who should be celebrating the Nag Hammadi discovery, the Church has been the least moved. Far from embracing this incredible new evidence, mainstream Christianity has openly dismissed its credibility, in the hopes of holding on forever to its familiar, yet misguided understanding of Jesus and his message. Since the beginning, this has been our way: We would rather cling to our familiar lies than embrace a strange truth, especially when we are intoxicated by the acquired taste of centuries-old fermented beliefs.

This could explain why "Truth" has never been able to find a foothold within our mainstream religions, communities, or cultures, and why it has instead struggled to survive on the sidelines, battling the demons of familiarity. While the majority simply accepts the human condition as a given, every so often, an individual comes along who threatens the known and unravels the mystery hidden behind it. For those who are willing to walk the solitary path, unafraid to be cast out by society, a lesser-known spiritual path has always existed. Perhaps there has never been another teacher who has spoken as much about this solitary path as Jesus, whose very purpose, reflected in essentially every verse of his teachings, was to isolate the individual from the crowd.

Jesus' teachings can easily be misinterpreted if we do not understand their intended audience. Throughout the centuries, we have been led to believe that Jesus was addressing the human community, serving his images as the "Savior of the World." However, there is no evidence from the scriptures supporting this assumption. In fact, there is not a single idea in all of Jesus' recorded verses that can directly benefit mankind as a whole, for a good reason. Jesus was a mystic who cared very little for the collective idea of humanity or trying to save it. He was a simple man rooted in the reality of the present moment, who would have been utterly incapable of deluding himself into believing that he was the only "Savior of the World."

Jesus was searching for individuals, fishing for men, to guide them toward their higher selves. He was willing to go against the deeply entrenched Jewish beliefs, whose dogmatic ways he had already dismissed as doomed, for the sake of those individuals.. There is no ambiguity in Jesus' assessment of the condition of his people when he says, "Follow me. Let the dead bury the dead."

Jesus spoke for one reason, and one reason alone: to liberate individuals from the illusionary world of dreams and desires that was smothering their intelligence and aliveness. For centuries, his people had been blissfully asleep in their daily routines, habits, and rituals, having grown accustomed to deriving pleasure from the fleeting comforts of life, while living in an eternal state of fear and uncertainty, detached from their original nature.

He was speaking to awaken individuals from their deep slumber of life, to shake their crumbling world in hopes of resurrecting something new within them. It is this internal cleansing process he was referring to when he said, "A grapevine has been planted outside of the father, but being unsound, it will be pulled up by its roots and destroyed."

In his usual poetic poise, Jesus was saying that Man's mind has taken over his life entirely, leaving no room for the silent contemplation of the eternal life dwelling within - an individual has to transcend this condition sooner or later.

Although Jesus was addressing the masses, he was speaking directly to the individual. He was fully aware that his teachings were not meant for all, and that eventually, only a handful would be able to grasp the sheer profundity of his message. He clarifies this himself in one of his finest verses: "Enter through the narrow gate. For wide is the gate and broad is the road that leads to destruction, and many enter through it. But small is the gate and narrow the path that leads to life, and only a few find it."

There is no such thing as a spiritual language. Language belongs to the worldly realm. It is only with the help of parables and allegories that we can attempt to capture, in words, any transcendental experience that is, by definition, beyond the grasp of human senses.

When a mystic like Jesus refers to something as the "kingdom of heaven," one can be certain that he is not talking about a "kingdom" or "heaven." He is alluding to something that is either too profound or too simple to be captured in words. As absurd as this may sound now, especially considering how grossly we have misinterpreted Jesus' teachings, the "kingdom of heaven," in all its glorious simplicity, is nothing but the eternal present moment.

While the present appears to us as a single fleeting moment, almost non-existential; in actuality, it is the only unchanging reality of life that is both eternal and complete. Jesus' "narrow path" is, quite literally, the undivided space that exists between two thoughts - the seat of the Self, and of all happenings.

Jesus was calling out to people, urging them to stop and reflect on this sacred realm of aliveness permeating everything, to which they had been totally oblivious. This is why, when asked, "When will the kingdom come?", he answers, "The kingdom is spread but people don't see it. It will not come by waiting for it. It will not be a matter of saying, 'here it is' or 'there it is.' Rather, the kingdom is spread out upon the earth, and men do not see it."

There is a vast difference between Jesus' idea of eternal life and the biblical interpretation of it. While Jesus was referring to an internal realm of aliveness accessible to us here and now, we have missed the subtlety of his message altogether by clinging to a purely imaginary "eternal life" in heaven, further widening the chasm that separates us from the truth. We have been saying all along that "eternal life" is in heaven and that Jesus alone holds the key to it, while Jesus himself said, "Don't believe it when people say it is here and it is there, for the kingdom of heaven is within you."

Jesus' idea of "eternal life" was nothing new. He was simply re-introducing a pearl of ancient, timeless wisdom in reminding his people of their forgotten identity - only in a much more forceful and authoritative manner. The central underlying theme in all of Jesus' sayings is this urgent message of getting back to the roots of one's being, to dwell in the truth of the present moment.

To this end, Jesus was vehemently against all distractions blocking an individual's path to freedom, including blind dogmatic beliefs and practices, binding family structures and attachments, and the meaningless pursuit of wealth and material comforts. He was against everything that threatened to take individuals deeper into the quagmire of life - further away from their true nature.

The most difficult thing to understand about Jesus is his revolutionary message, alien to all things people were capable of comprehending. Walking the solitary path doesn't mean running away from life; however, it does ask one to step away from everything familiar to pursue an unknown path to freedom. Although the idea of detachment is simple enough to understand, pursuing it is anything but easy.

It only takes a few steps of descending into our inner world of thoughts and memories to see that everything we know about ourselves comes from the people around us. As a human community, all we have been doing is borrowing ideas and making them our own. Our minds are nothing more than a random collection of fears and desires gathered from here and there, swirling in an ever-changing entanglement of unresolved emotions.

As an awakened man, Jesus was fully aware that only an individual, detached from his social conditioning, can explore the hidden mysteries of life. Truth can find its expression inside the heart of a blind man, a rich or a poor man, a saint or a sinner, but it cannot take root when the individual is missing. As he has so eloquently put it, "Show me the stone which the builders have rejected. That one is the cornerstone."

Words are like empty cups; they can hold many things at the same time. By the very nature of their limitation they are, at best, a symbolic reference to reality, and never an actual representation of it. While many will hear the words, only a few, adept at seeing beyond their literal meaning, can understand their true purpose. For every right way of deciphering the secret language of words, there are countless ways of getting them wrong. A case in point is biblical theology, which has mutilated Jesus' words beyond recognition simply by interpreting them literally.

Using the parable of a sower, Jesus explains how easily one can miss those precious life-altering gems of wisdom hidden in words: "Now the sower went out, took a handful of seeds, and scattered them. Some fell on the road; the birds came and gathered them up. Others fell on the rock and did not take root. Some fell on the thorns, and some were eaten by worms. A few fell on good soil and produced fruit in great abundance."

Jesus was searching for a select few capable of hearing him, not through the noise of their conditioned minds but through the silence of their untainted spirits. Despite being aware that most would altogether misunderstand him, he persists, saying, "Those who have ears will hear, and those who have eyes will see."

Although brief, in his entire lifetime of teaching, Jesus managed to attract only a handful of serious followers - twelve, to be precise. Far from being a revered, well-known figure, he was easily one of the most misunderstood, ridiculed, and despised individuals of his time; and yet, ironically, over the years, more than two billion individuals have managed to pass through his narrow gate, prompting the question: How did this rebellious hermit's extraordinarily hard to understand

and even harder to practice message become so popular?

To find the answer, we have to look no further than our distorted biblical interpretation of Jesus' life and message. It was never the real Jesus or his revolutionary teachings that spread around the world. We simply fell in love with our own glorified image of Jesus, settling for a fabricated, diluted form of his teachings whose razor-sharp edges, capable of cutting through centuries of religious dogmatism, were dulled to a point beyond recognition.

Allegorical phrases such as "listening to silence," "seeing in darkness," "being born again," and "walking on water," are all common expressions describing one's inward spiritual journey; they mean nothing in the outer physical world. When interpreted literally, either out of ignorance or to serve a misguided purpose, these very same phrases, meant to awaken the human spirit, can just as easily plunge it into superstitious slumber.

A recurring theme in Jesus' teachings, on which rests the foundation of the Christian faith, is the Father and Son analogy. In various contexts, Jesus circles back to this idea again and again: "You are the sons of the living father;" "I am he who exists from the undivided. I was given some of the things of my father;" and "The kingdom of the father is spread out upon the earth, and men do not see it."

Not surprisingly, we have taken this analogy entirely out of context to concoct an imaginary abstraction of the holy trinity made up of the Father, the Son, and the Holy Ghost. If it can be shown that Jesus was using these words figuratively, our traditional interpretation would fall flat on its face.

We only have to be reminded that Jesus taught in parables. Despite speaking in a common, easy-to-understand, worldly language, he was referring to something far more existential than the human experience. He was using the words "father" and "son," in their most simplistic sense, to describe the relationship that exists between universal consciousness supporting everything and the individual human life emanating from it, between the source and its creation.

This is why Jesus says, "You are made in the image of the father," which means that the separation we experience as individuals is only a matter of perception, for at the center of it all, we are one. It is this oneness of life he was referring to when he said, "I am the only way."

As a realized man, Jesus often spoke in first person, identifying himself fully with the Truth he had come to discover within him. This is what gives his teachings that characteristic, unmistakable air of authority. "It is I who am the light which is above them all. It is I who am the all. From me did the all come forth, and unto me did the all extend. Split a piece of wood, and I am there. Lift up the stone, and you will find me there."

Jesus could speak like this, referring to himself as the ultimate Truth, not because he was a messenger of God sent to save humanity, but only because he was a self-realized man fully aware of the true nature of his being. When Jesus says, "I am the light, I am the way, and I am the only Truth," he isn't speaking in his capacity as an individual, but as the voice of that undivided realm of aliveness he was now one with.

Unable to make a simple distinction between Jesus the man and his message, we have grossly mis-interpreted his first-person narrative as divine authority ordained from God to make him an end unto himself, reducing his life's work to nothing more than mildly amusing hypnotic sermons reverberating the hallowed chambers of our glorified faith.

ROUND PEG IN A SQUARE HOLE

Words are like ladders. They can be used either to climb to heights of clarity and wisdom or descend to the depths of chaos and confusion. In the hands of an ambitious, world-conquering ideology, the inspirational and illuminating words of Jesus became tools of dominance and suppression. The very same words meant to liberate humanity were instead used to subdue its free spirit.

For more than a thousand years, the Church wielded Jesus' words like a Roman whip, to command and control. We can think of very few other institutions that have used as much brute force to spread their message. Only a blunted Roman logic could have assumed that it can spread Jesus' true message around the world by simply carving his name into people's hearts, even if it meant using a sword to accomplish it.

The power-hungry philosophy of the Church, however, had failed to understand one fundamental law of existence: that love and force can never dwell in the same house - when one enters, the other has to leave. When the Roman force entered early Christianity, Jesus quietly deserted it. Since then, Christianity has been a religion, hinging more on the death and resurrection of Jesus than the mystical beauty and fragrance of his original teachings.

With our every attempt to force people to accept Jesus as the savior, we have, in fact, alienated them from the possibility of understanding and internalizing his true message. By assuming that Jesus is a divine being altogether different from us, we have conveniently diverted attention away from his teachings and their true intended purpose. To call Jesus the only begotten "Son of God" is an insult to both humanity and existence. Why should existence be such a miser and create just one Jesus, when it could have just as easily created many more? It's as though, after creating this one special man, it simply forgot how to do it again.

For argument's sake, if we accept that only one such man was ever created, the question is: Why did existence break away from its normal process of creation to produce such an anomaly in the first place? Even a basic understanding of life reveals that creation never picks and chooses from its work. Life does not know how to make a distinction between special and ordinary. In the eyes of creation, either everything is special, or nothing is.

Jesus was just an ordinary man who had found something profound and was urging people to look for it within themselves. No one has been able to explain the difference between Jesus and those around him better than Jesus himself.

There is an intriguing passage in the Gnostic Gospel of Thomas, where Jesus asks his disciples to compare him to someone and tell him who he is like. Simon Peter says that he is like a righteous angel. Matthew compares him to a wise philosopher. Thomas says, "Master, my mouth is wholly incapable of describing you." To this Jesus replies, "I am not your master, for you have drunk and become intoxicated from the bubbling spring which I have measured out."

Here, Jesus reveals something significant. Far from recognizing himself as a divine being or the "Son of God," he is refusing to even call himself their master. He tells them that by striving to understand his teachings and experience the Truth he has been guiding them to, they have become like him.

In a way, Jesus is saying that all those who drink from the wellspring of eternal life become like him. Eternal life is not some otherworldly, esoteric spiritual concept, but a far more realistic, attainable inner experience. He is saying the exact same thing Buddha, Muhammad, and many other awakened teachers have said; the Truth we seek is within us.

Jesus isn't saying that he was sent to save our souls and take them to heaven. He is telling us that by understanding and practicing his spiritual teachings, we can have an internal experience of eternal life right here on earth, in this very lifetime. He is pointing to the same ancient spiritual process through which Gautama became Buddha, Abu al Qasim became Muhammad, and he himself became Christ, the anointed one.

Despite centuries of scriptural alteration and misrepresentation, Jesus is still a round peg in a square biblical hole. The stark contrast in the personalities of Jesus and other biblical characters is clearly evident. While the anthropomorphic God of the Bible is jealous, angry, and judgmental, Jesus is profound and insightful. While the Bible God rants in authoritative prose, Jesus unravels his mysteries in poetic parables. To communicate his message, the Bible God commands and punishes, while the human Jesus teaches and guides.

The Gnostic Gospels reveal a remarkably human Jesus who shares a complex, intricate relationship with his disciples. Unlike the biblical God who is screaming from the rooftops and looking down upon lesser mortals, Jesus is engaged in a deep and meaningful conversation with his disciples. He answers their questions, clears their path of obstacles, and guides them toward spiritual awakening.

As a mystic and a teacher, Jesus' words mean something altogether different from what is implied in the Bible. When Jesus says, "I shall give you what no eye has seen, what no ear has heard, what no hand has touched, and what has never occurred to the human mind," he is talking about something tangible and real, which can only be experienced within. He is talking about the ultimate purpose of human life - finding the purest part of one's being.

The human mind is not a reality, but a condition, mystics have always maintained. Through the power of our desires, we accumulate thoughts and become entangled in their web of ideas. The mind grows over us like a creeper, to eventually block out the ability to perceive our pure, unblemished Self. Our mind is made up of layers and layers of accumulated thoughts that are always moving and changing. With no firm ground on which to settle, they are in a state of eternal disturbance.

Compared to all other creatures of existence, we humans are the most restless, for we have made an occupation out of thinking. As a species, we suffer from excessive thinking, the symptoms of which are fear and uncertainty. This is why Jesus says, "The foxes have their holes and the birds have their nests, but the son of man has no place to lay his head and rest."

However mystical and otherworldly Jesus' words may sound, he is still talking about a real experience one can have. He is not talking about an imaginary eternal life in heaven that can be enjoyed only after death. He is neither asking us to blindly believe in him nor is he condemning our ordinary human lives as sin. While we have been praying, fasting, giving alms, and building churches and cathedrals in his name, he isn't asking for any of this. He is only offering a possibility.

Having had the ultimate experience an individual can ever hope to have, Jesus was guiding people to the same abode of internal bliss and wonder he was in. He was offering a path beyond the constant noise and disturbance of the mind, to an internal realm of peace and certainty. He was drawing people's attention away from their troubled pasts and ambitious futures to the reality of the present moment. For lack of a better expression, he calls this realm, "the kingdom of heaven" without realizing just how political that sounded.

Of all the mistakes Jesus could have avoided as a fiery young teacher, this might have well been his biggest. It isn't hard to imagine how different Jesus' life and death would have been, or how different Christianity might have been as a religion if only he hadn't used the words "kingdom" and "heaven" - possibly two of the most heavily loaded words in the human vocabulary.

Of the many things that drew people to Christianity, Jesus' original message was not one of them. The deeply insightful, spiritual teachings of Jesus had always been just beyond the interpretation of the general population. In fact, it is only by rejecting Jesus' hard-to-grasp message - by diluting his teachings altogether, that we have been able to transform his simple message into a widespread religious phenomenon.

On the surface, Jesus might appear to be the main draw of the Christian faith, but in reality, he is just one of many cogs in the wheel of Christian machinery. The single most important event that altered the functioning DNA of Christianity was Constantine's endorsement which exalted it to an unparalleled status.

What, up until then, was a ridiculed, often persecuted fringe religious movement, had suddenly become a force to be reckoned with. Empowered by the new ambitious Roman blood, the well-oiled machine of the Church advanced, consuming everything in its path. Hell-bent on imposing its newfound way of life, it began settling scores with all its old adversaries, particularly the Jews.

Intoxicated by the lust for power and blinded by its desire for world dominance, the Church was no longer content in being that Jewish spiritual tree standing in some obscure corner of Jerusalem, offering shade and respite to the spiritually parched. Instead, it aimed to be the sky, and claim everything under it as its own.

However, the faithful insiders held a very different view of the Church, unable to see from the outside. They believed that it drew people by the millions for the hope it provided, without which they would all be lost. They saw the Church as a warm, comforting refuge - a beacon of light for all those aimlessly wandering the cold, dark wilderness of life. Their faith promised eternal life in heaven and provided a moral framework for living a better life here on earth. They believed that without this divine compass to show the difference between right and wrong, humanity would lose its sense of direction and fall into chaos and despair.

Even if we assume all this to be true, there is still nothing unique about this promise. Virtually every other religion assures its believers the very same thing.

What separated Christianity from other religions wasn't its unique message, but how it went about propagating it. While other religions take a more passive approach to introducing people to their faiths, the new Roman Church was actively and aggressively organizing itself to draw every last bystander into its circle of beliefs.

Over time, people became so used to this behavior, they simply assumed that "spreading the faith" is the primary objective of religion. Little did they know that if there is one thing that can never be imposed from the outside, it is religion. Forcing one's religious beliefs onto others is a violation of the rights of the human spirit, and we have, for far too long, on a scale unconscionable, been guilty of committing this mistake.

Religiousness is a rare, fragrant flower blossoming on the highest branch of the tree of life. It arises as an inner longing within an individual, as a quest for something greater that can complete them. It is a delicate, fleeting emotion for which an individual has to be open and ready. Even the slightest use of force or coercion with the intention of imposition shatters it.

The unprecedented growth and expansion of a religion, with its disdain for all other belief systems, compels one to ask the question, "What exactly is the purpose of religion?" Is it to address the spiritual needs of an individual looking for answers to the most important questions of life; or is it to cleverly and meticulously organize itself, to draw as many individuals as possible into its circle of influence, claiming greatness solely by the sheer scale and size of its operations? The Church measured its success, not by how well it managed to help an individual understand the spiritual teachings of Jesus, but by how far and wide it was able to expand its religious empire.

The Church, right from the beginning, operated less like a religion and more like a medieval kingdom obsessed with conquest and expansion, with its entire basis of existence centered around power and control. Interwoven firmly into the fabric of its religious theology and organizational structure, the slogan "spread the faith" became Christendom's war cry to rid the world of its rich spiritual diversity, to replace it all with its one God-ordained religion.

The extent to which the idea of expansion was burrowed into our human psyche is re-asserted by the fact that even to this day, we truly believe that of all the virtues, "spreading the faith" is the most Christian. To further its expansion goals, the Church turned us into its personal mouthpieces, and we didn't even care to complain. Perhaps that is the advantage of having God on your side - to defend your ambitions and actions.

We have always believed that "spreading the faith" is one of Jesus' original instructions to us. After coming out of his long spiritual hibernation and addressing the multitude gathered around him for the first time, Jesus is reported to have said, "The kingdom of heaven is here, share the good news."

There is no reason to doubt whether Jesus actually said this or not. After all, he was now an awakened man sharing the good news of his realization and naturally wanting as many as possible to know about it. It is easy to conclude that we are obsessed with the idea of "spreading the message" because it is what we were instructed to do. We have simply been following in the footsteps of Jesus.

However, there is a big difference between Jesus saying "share the good news" and the Church urging us to "spread the faith." Jesus' "Good News" isn't just a religious philosophy - it is an actual inner spiritual experience an individual can strive for and attain. On the other hand, the biblical theology, upon which the foundation of Christianity rests, is a random assortment of beliefs, mostly derived from an erroneous interpretation of an ancient culture - a three-thousand-year-old biblical porridge, peppered with some Jesus sayings, and served on a cold and somber platter of guilt.

THE GAMES WE PLAY

The central tenet of the Jewish Bible is the belief that God has been sending messiahs to speak on his behalf - that he uses prophets, literally "spokesmen of God," to command, control, and ultimately guide his chosen people toward him. Abraham, Moses, Jeremiah, Ezekiel, David, and Jesus have all been identified as Jewish prophets sent by God to proclaim his message. Judaism has maintained this tradition for well over four thousand years, adding a new messiah every few hundred years or so to its long list of God's messengers.

This monotheistic belief in one God and his messengers is the bloodline of the Jewish religion. The Jews would never accept a prophet who didn't directly come from this lineage of ancient prophetic tradition. Once accepted, such a prophet's word is taken to be absolute and unquestionable. Rejecting a proclaimed prophet's authority was considered blasphemy against God and, under Jewish law, punishable by death.

Unlike polytheistic religions that believe in many gods, the Jewish faith accepted nothing less than total allegiance and submission to this one God and his divine will. By virtue of being born a Jew or accepting the faith by choice, an individual was bound to Jewish religious laws, customs, and traditions for life.

It isn't surprising how eerily similar all of this is to how Christianity functions. The Christian faith isn't just gently resting on the broad foundations of Judaism - the Jewish story is carved into every brick. Christianity doesn't just share Jewish roots; Judaism's living sap flows through every branch, leaf, flower, and fruit of the Christian tree.

Even after thousands of years of the monotheistic prophetic tradition, the questions, "Who is God, who are his prophets, and what exactly is their purpose?" still remain unanswered. Even with a simple application of logic, we can clearly see that there is something odd about the idea of God sending messengers to speak on his behalf.

When talking about God, it is easy to forget that we are referring to "The God" - the mighty, all-powerful creator of the earth, sky, and everything in between - a being who has the power to breathe life into someone or take it away - the master of time, creation, and life itself. Now, why would such an omnipotent, omnipresent God leave the rest of his creation alone to especially communicate with Man? We are yet to convincingly answer this question.

The God of the Bible chooses to put Man right at the center of his creation, so much so that he reduces all other creatures to a subservient position. For some unknown reason, this biblical God is obsessed with Man. Apparently, his favorite pastime is watching human beings all day, judging them by arbitrary ideas of right and wrong, to reward or punish them accordingly.

The Bible God is often depicted as pompous, arrogant, and blatantly immoral. Every time he makes an appearance to say something, he comes across less like a divine being and more like a glorified version of the male ego. Theists would argue that as ordinary mortals, we are nowhere near capable of questioning God and his ways - God is beyond the comprehension of ordinary minds, and any judgment of his character is simply a reflection of our own limitations. To a certain extent, this is true, but as human beings, we at least know how to recognize our own kind. We might struggle to identify the mysterious qualities of this God, but we certainly know what a human ego sounds and feels like.

Even from a mile away, the Bible God can be unmistakably recognized by his distinct male ego. We might not be able to directly look into the mind of this God, but we can certainly judge him by his actions. With one look at the human race and the confused state he has left his chosen people in, we can come to a reasonable conclusion that the Bible God, if he is real, is either intentionally cruel or, by nature, insensitive.

If God loved Man so much, why didn't he create him perfect the first time around? Why did he have to send a messenger to remind him that he was lost? And, of all the available creatures of existence available to him, why would he send a man to do the job, knowing well that we human beings have trouble trusting our own kind? Unable to foresee the inevitable tragedy, he sends his only son to the Jews, who looks and talks just like them, armed with nothing but his message.

What kind of God would have trouble predicting the brutal, agonizing death of his human messenger in the hands of his own children? He could have just as easily considered a talking pony for the job, which would have at least attracted the attention of many more. Without any ego or self-interest issues, a pony would have been easier for people to trust. And, not knowing how to crucify it, the Romans would have probably spared its life.

If this idea sounds childish and insulting, then so does the belief that God loved human beings so much that he sacrificed his only son to atone for their sins. Any civilized human would understand that it is unjust and immoral to punish someone for a crime they have not committed. And yet, this all-knowing God chooses to sacrifice his perfectly good son for the sake of his lost children. If we can somehow visualize this divine philosophy of the Bible God, it would probably look like someone gnawing on their perfectly healthy fingers in the hopes of saving their rotting feet.

When we are able to move beyond the dogmatic belief that prophets are messengers sent by God, we can begin to explore the hidden truth behind their stories. It is certain that individuals like Buddha, Jesus, Abraham, and Moses are not wholly fictional characters. No religion, however powerful or organized, can pull human beings out of thin air and expect millions of people to accept and follow them. A purely fictional character not rooted in reality can stay relevant only for so long. Only truth has the power to stand the test of time and stay alive, even when buried deep under the rubble of ignorance.

Despite successful attempts to hijack the lives of these extraordinary individuals, their timeless wisdom and truth shine through the brick walls of misunderstanding to draw people's attention. If there wasn't any truth to the life of Jesus, despite our best attempts to keep him relevant, we would have forgotten him by now.

We can distort the facts of an individual's life to a point beyond recognition, but we can never build the supporting structures of faith on the shoulders of a purely imaginary figure. Without Jesus' truth to hold it all together, Christianity would have disintegrated a long time ago.

While we have regarded Jesus' divinity to be his ultimate truth, his teachings reveal something entirely different. The words and actions of Jesus, far from supporting traditional beliefs, are, in fact, vehemently opposed to them. Just like his predecessors Abraham and Moses, Jesus was questioning the orthodox Jewish belief system that had stifled individual freedom. His rebellious nature, coupled with spiritual insight, is what separated Jesus from others - the same qualities that separated any messiah from ordinary men.

While most of us are content settling for the familiar comforts life offers, a few rare individuals are willing to settle for nothing less than the truth. One of the essential prerequisites for becoming a spiritually self-realized individual, or as we have called them "messiahs," is the courage to break away from one's deep social and cultural conditioning.

In this sense, Jesus, Buddha, and Muhammad are not religious leaders, but religious rebels who fought against the orthodox belief systems they were born into. Like so many others, if they had been obedient adherents of their faiths, we would not have cared to remember them. Jews were curious about Jesus not because he was a shining example of a perfect Jew, but only because he had branched off to find his own truth.

For a religion professing to be the sole gateway to heaven, any individual claiming to be a "Messenger of God" poses a direct threat to its existence. Such an individual should either be eliminated, or in a circumstance where that is not possible, be brought inside its religious walls as a Messiah sanctioned by its one God.

This is how men like Jesus, Abraham, and Moses eventually ended up inside the very same belief systems they were fighting against. This monotheistic religious game between God, his messengers, and his people, going on for thousands of years, has been the single biggest source of conflict on earth, spilling enough blood to turn the oceans red.

Who is this violent, bloodthirsty God responsible for plunging the human race into the dark ages? Where did this Abrahamic God, claiming to be the Father of all, come from? Did he actually create us and everything else in his image, as the Bible claims, or did we create him in our image? Is Man a game played by God, or is God a game played by Man?

In all these years, we have yet to come across a single conclusive piece of evidence supporting the existence of an anthropomorphic God who listens to and responds to our needs, except for a belief that he does. Some would argue that just because we have not conclusively proven the presence of God does not imply that we have proven his absence. It isn't hard to see why such an argument is inherently flawed. Based on our understanding of the natural world and our interaction with it, we can reasonably conclude that there are no flying pigs. Any argument suggesting that they might, after all, exist and we have only yet to see them is childish at best.

So far, based on all that we know, we can safely conclude that there is no such mythical being in the sky who is particularly interested in human affairs. The idea of "God" might just be a figment of our imagination, and possibly, one of our biggest psychological stumbling blocks. Since time immemorial, Man has used God as a religious bogeyman to control the masses. Religion isn't so much a story of God and his divine plans as much as it is a story of Man and his quest for power and control.

Just because we are choosing to deny the existence of a personal human-like God who is nothing more than a projection of our own self-image, doesn't mean that we are denying the presence of such higher spiritual qualities as love, compassion, beauty, bliss, and goodness, which are beyond the comprehension of the human mind.

Man's search has never been for God or heaven, but instead, for a pure, undivided perception of life. The best of all we have been searching for is already interwoven into the fabric of our human lives - fully realizing this has been our only challenge. This is why Jesus says, "The kingdom of God is within you; seek and you shall find it." Buddha's Nirvana, the ultimate experience an individual can hope to have, is simply a realization of inner "Nothingness" - the purest part of one's being.

Prophets and messiahs have neither referred to themselves as gods nor have they been interested in guiding people toward heaven. They have only spoken about a divine, transcendental realm dwelling within us, waiting to be discovered. In the name of God, knowingly or unknowingly, we have separated ourselves from our search. At the level of thoughts and ideas, religion appears to offer a direct path to individual liberation, but often, it is the single biggest obstacle standing between Man and his highest possibility.

Once in a while, a man like Jesus comes along who threatens to turn this religious game on its head. He stands firm in his own understanding of life, asserting a simple existential fact: that to be fully human is to be divine. He draws people's attention away from God and religion and onto themselves. He proclaims with utmost certainty that the divine cannot exist on the outside; for all experiences are human, especially the ones we call "religious."

Men like Jesus and Buddha remind us that Man and God are two ends of the same rope. We cannot separate a human being from their divinity any more than we can separate a flower from its beauty. To say that there is an anthropomorphic God somewhere beyond the worldly realm who has absolute power over human lives is an insult to humanity, its intelligence and everything it represents. Even if such a non-physical, transcendental being as "God" were to be real, there is no reason why, of all the different creatures of existence, he should choose to be so human-like.

"God" - if we have to even use that word - being the source of all things, has to be formless, timeless, and devoid of all qualities, human or any other. He has to be everywhere, in all things, and at all times. He cannot judge, question, choose, or take sides, and especially like the Bible God, he cannot punish, reward, or sacrifice someone. By the very definition, "God" cannot be a noun. The only thing in existence that can come close to such a qualitative definition of God, is consciousness. If there is indeed a God, he resides within each and every being as a dormant possibility.

As creatures bound to the physicality of life, we are conditioned to look at everything through the narrow keyhole of our senses. Owing to this limitation, we perceive the world around us only in bits and pieces, and never in its totality. By the very nature of our perception, which is designed to recognize change, we cannot perceive something that is eternally present, complete, and unchanging. In this sense, the only thing that is truly hidden from us is our own pure state of being.

Unable to grasp the eternal, undivided nature of our being, we have been searching for life's meaning in ephemeral things outside of ourselves. No matter how hard we try to make sense of the world around us, the emptiness of not knowing who we are has followed us like a shadow. There has always been a huge gap between who we are and what we know about ourselves. Taking advantage of this void in human perception, religions have filled humanity's mind with all kinds of superficial ideas of God, his messengers, heaven, and hell.

Messiahs neither suddenly drop from heaven, nor are they figments of religious imagination. They are examples of human perfection chiseled out of ordinary lives through a process of self-discovery. Prophets, during their lifetimes, are almost always ridiculed and rejected by the majority. It is only much later, usually decades after their death, that they are recognized for their unusual wisdom and exalted to the status of a prophet.

Both the profundity of his message and the guilt of his people go hand in hand in transforming a simple human teacher into a "Messenger of God." In the case of Jesus, both the magnanimity of his message and the guilt of its rejection stirred people's emotions in unimaginable ways, elevating him all the way to the status of the "Son of God."

Even to this day, no other emotion draws people to Jesus like guilt. This is the reason why, when we walk into a church, instead of encountering a serene, inviting spiritual teacher, we are greeted by a young man hanging on a cross.

THE CAULDRON OF CONFLICTS

It is hard to predict what would come out of a cauldron of repressed human emotions when an orthodox religion, a profound mystic, a mighty empire, and a distraught community are all thrown into the mix. Yet, we do know that Christianity emerged from precisely one such environment. It is easy to forget that Christianity took its first baby steps and developed its defining beliefs, rituals, and traditions at a time when people still believed that women were an inferior race and sickness was caused by evil spirits.

Early Christianity drew its nourishment from the chaotic, muddy waters of a deeply religious Jerusalem, where everyday events were explained, not by logic or reasoning but by superstitious beliefs of a majority that could neither read nor write.

When a community lacks the basic awareness to process critical information that could expand its understanding of life, it becomes enslaved to its collective social habits and conditionings. Its ability to grasp certain simple, universal truths of life is limited to the social norms dictated by its immediate surroundings.

An intellectually stagnated environment presents ideal conditions for a clever and crafty few to thrive by feeding on the ignorance of the many. This may be why the ancient and timeless practice of mysticism has not flourished within any of our mainstream human societies or cultures and has had to retreat deep into the caves, mountains, and deserts of the world, far away from human civilization.

The path to Truth has always been narrow, open only to those willing to break free from the quagmire of social conditioning. Mankind, in general, has lived under some form of mutually accepted superstition, with these beliefs becoming increasingly strange the farther we go back in time. Almost all of these superstitions revolve around two fundamental human emotions: fear and greed.

There was a time, not too long ago, when people believed that all natural phenomena such as ocean waves, eclipses, thunder and lightning, sickness and death, were caused by mysterious forces beyond the human realm. The further we delve into our past, the more mysterious these sources become, with an all-powerful God at the center, filling the gaps in human understanding.

Over time, with the aid of science and reasoning, mankind has been able to better explain the cause-and-effect relationships between events more effectively. In fact, if humanity has matured in any way throughout the years, it has primarily done so mainly by bringing the divine and mysterious force from the high heavens down to the level of human understanding. Although science may still be far from answering some of life's most crucial questions, by revealing the underlying order within the universe, it has eliminated the notion of a God who plays dice.

Without the scientific awareness needed to logically piece together events and experiences, early human societies viewed their fortunes and misfortunes not as part of the ebb and flow of one indivisible life, but as independent and disconnected events randomly thrust upon them by an unknown external force. They arrived at an overly simplistic conclusion that all good things came from God, while the devil was responsible for their woes.

It's not surprising that the life and message of a simple man like Jesus, who had discovered the same underlying oneness of life that modern science has reaffirmed with each new discovery, was completely misunderstood. We were unable to see that an ordinary human being, one of our own, could attain unusual heights of clarity and wisdom simply by fully understanding life. Our deeply conditioned minds were incapable of recognizing Jesus for who he truly was. We only saw him in the way our limited understanding of life allowed us to - as the 'Son of God,' sent as a sacrifice to save our lost souls.

Often, it is the background against which an image is viewed that shapes its defining characteristics. This is true even more so in the case of Jesus. Our biblical image of Jesus was primarily shaped by the looming backdrop of Jerusalem. If we were to remove Jerusalem from the picture, we would have a vastly different image of Jesus. In fact, it would not be an exaggeration to say that the single biggest difference between Jesus and Buddha is Jerusalem.

Jerusalem, a small, ancient hilltop city in the Judean desert, was at the center of one of the most bitter religious conflicts. Regarded as the most sacred site by Jews, Muslims, and Christians alike, Jerusalem was a religious fault line running through the heartland of Jewish sentiments. This fault line was carved by the power struggle between two colossal tectonic plates of politics and religion.

Over the centuries, several mighty empires of the world, including the Babylonians, Romans, Persians, Arabs, and Egyptians, have attacked, conquered, and ruled over this ancient city. For more than three thousand years, the bone of contention in Jerusalem has been a thirty-five-acre compound called the Temple Mount - the site where King David's son Solomon built the first temple.

Jesus arrived in Jerusalem during one of its busiest times of the year. Jews from all over Judea had gathered in the city to celebrate Passover - a seven-day Jewish festival commemorating their exodus from Egyptian slavery more than a thousand years earlier.

Contrary to how the Bible recounts it, Jesus did not triumphantly ride into Jerusalem on a donkey to an arousing reception of cheering crowds. In all probability, he walked barefoot from Galilee to Jerusalem along with a handful of his followers, unaware that he would be walking through those crumbling stone gates of Jerusalem one last time.

Jesus entered Jerusalem, not as the king of the Jews, but as a breath of fresh air to a troubled region saturated in chaos and religious decay. Unlike the crowds that had gathered there to observe Passover, admire its ancient Jewish temples, or trade in its sprawling markets, Jesus came with a different purpose. He came from a place of internal serenity, unfamiliar to the noisy, crowded streets of Jerusalem, bringing to the Jews an even stranger message, whose grandeur and beauty they were unable to comprehend.

Having spent the best part of his adult life in the company of mystics, Jesus gathered precious seeds of spiritual wisdom that he scattered wherever he went. He made this long trip to Jerusalem, hoping to see some of those seeds take root in the parched desert sands. However, his hope was futile.

The single biggest casualty of prolonged violence and unrest within any society is individual freedom and its vibrant possibilities. Individuality, a sapling of still waters, does well in conditions of peace and stability, but struggles and eventually withers away in a turbid atmosphere of constant change and uncertainty.

The Jews of first-century Jerusalem, amidst an unrelenting religious and social upheaval, had sacrificed their higher faculties of individuality in exchange for a collective hive mind that buzzed around a common set of beliefs, aimed mostly at preserving their only known way of life. At a time when their homeland was under siege by an alien race that neither cared for the dignity of their living nor respected the sanctity of their dead, nothing was more important than sticking together. Unaware of this volatile state of affairs and the complex dynamics at play, a young and naive Jesus, shielded by truth alone, steps into Jerusalem's thick, suffocating smog of conflicting ideologies.

Jesus, as a man, could not have been more different from the inhabitants of Jerusalem. After years of passionate searching for Truth - time spent in silence and solitude - far from the noise and chaos of mainstream society - he had forgotten just how different he had become from his fellow Jews.

Jesus had become a world unto himself, needing little from those around him. And yet, something had driven him toward those large human congregations. Perhaps it was a primordial instinct to connect and share his newfound realization, or maybe he was simply acting on that invisible human impulse that so often compels us to love, forgive, and side with truth, even when some part of us knows that we are destined to be doomed in its service.

If we are the sum total of all our influences, then Jesus, nourished by the best spiritual wisdom in the womb of silence and stillness, must have been vastly different from the first-century Jews of Jerusalem. They grew up in an intellectually stifling environment of fear and suspicion, relying solely on a thousand-year-old belief system as their only source of spiritual nourishment.

Raised by a living spiritual path, Jesus had transcended the base desires plaguing humanity, including the Jews of Jerusalem. Like the Buddha, he had become utterly incorruptible - free of blind beliefs, meaningless desires, and imaginary fears that had driven the inhabitants of Jerusalem insane.

It was either love or madness that had brought Jesus to their midst in the hopes of bridging that wide chasm of "suspicion of all things new" - an idea interwoven into the very fabric of Jewish society by centuries of social and religious conditioning.

Jesus had put himself in the middle of this sea of humanity to wake people up from their deep social slumber and reintroduce them to their higher selves. He was unaware that his spiritually illiterate Jewish brothers, in their misplaced sense of morality, would rather shred him to pieces than question the biblical orthodoxy that clouded their judgment. They were wary and cynical of all things rooted in reality, especially a fully realized man like Jesus.

Forged by contrasting forces of nature and divided by habits, influences, and understandings of life, an enlightened Jesus and the Jews of Jerusalem had become two distinct species, sharing only the most basic gifts of life. Like any two creatures clinging to different branches of life, they could acknowledge each other's passion for life but could not understand their divergent paths and destinations. Their conversation was like a bird and an insect in the dark wilderness of life, hearing each other, but unable to make sense of what each was trying to say.

Jesus expresses disappointment in his fellow human beings' inability to recognize him for what he truly represents. He struggles to understand how his own species, whom he calls "the sons of the living light, the very salt of the earth," are wandering aimlessly, chasing empty desires and missing obvious truths that could at once set them free.

Conditioned for centuries to look up to the heavens for all their answers, the Jews of Jerusalem simply could not wrap their heads around Jesus' spiritual interpretation of their "Kingdom of Heaven." Their understanding of such a kingdom could not have been any more different from that of Jesus.

For over a millennium, the Jewish mind accepted the idea of a literal, physical kingdom of heaven where their God would sit on a throne to reign over them as their king. They awaited the arrival of their messiah who would lead them to their promised land of eternal peace and abundance, away from persecution and injustice. The Jews, who were deeply invested in such an idea, had issues with Jesus' unusual interpretation of their most cherished vision.

The Jews struggled to understand Jesus because he didn't support their traditional beliefs, or offer outlandish promises. However mystical and other-worldly Jesus' words may have sounded, he was still a man firmly rooted in reality. He had come to the Jews to offer a real possibility of finding something immensely meaningful, not somewhere outside, but within them, that could set their afflicted spirits free.

The Jewish mind was complicated by centuries of religious conditioning, expecting the kingdom to arrive in an unmistakable earth-shattering blaze of thunder and lightning. They were unable to comprehend the remarkable simplicity of Jesus' message, and the divide between them was much wider than he had imagined. Despite using the same words and referring to the same thing, the Jews of Jerusalem and an awakened Jesus were looking in two entirely different directions. While Jesus was trying to point them toward the inner treasures of life within themselves, their gaze was firmly set on the outside.

Physically, the Jews were close enough to feel the sincerity in Jesus' breath and conviction in his words, but intellectually, they might as well have been on another planet. Even when willing to pay the ultimate price, Jesus was unable to bridge the gap between them; they were separated by the most vicious of dividers - truth.

For a majority of the Jews, Jesus was the worst thing that could have happened to them, although it would be a long time before they fully realized this. When Jesus offered them his radical message, they thought they were being presented with a choice between their familiar way of life and something strange and new. Little did they know that when dealing with a man like Jesus - existence's highest expression of Truth - choice is simply an illusion.

While a lie can awkwardly hop on one leg and get by, the dignity of truth lies in being firmly rooted in reality on both legs. Truth has two sides: the visible and the hidden. Jesus offered the Jews a choice to either accept or reject him, but his spiritual verses had already begun writing the first of the last few chapters of the traditional Jewish way of life.

Accepting or rejecting Jesus wasn't a choice for the Jews, but a final verdict on their way of life. It wasn't a coincidence that Jesus was a Jew who landed in Jerusalem at Passover. Truth seemed to have been plotting against the Jewish orthodoxy, waiting for the right time to strike. Jerusalem just happened to be the right place, Passover the right occasion, and Jesus the perfect man for the job.

Jesus' life had been a preparation for this brief encounter with the Jews - not in any mysterious or divine sense, but in the sense that one extraordinary event can define everything about an individual. From the beginning, Jesus' individuality rebelled against Judaism's rigid orthodoxy, created by a clever few for the ignorant many, at the cost of the individual.

Jesus had found his teacher in John, a locust-eating, half-naked, enlightened hermit on the outskirts of everything he was familiar with. Jesus' unseen blueprint of life, which we call destiny, included being born a Jew and eventually returning to his people with a renewed understanding of life. While he was in Jerusalem to plant spiritual seeds of wisdom, the invisible hand guiding him was also using him to pull out some overgrown religious weeds.

Looking into the face of truth is like staring into a still lake. Before we are able to see its hidden mysteries, we must confront our own distorted reflections. The story of Jesus is that truth, which humanity exposed by revealing its dark underbelly of intolerance. While we have been ready to blame the Jews for rejecting Jesus, we have conveniently chosen to ignore humanity's long history of misunderstanding men like him.

"Understanding" is another word for the art of putting oneself in the shoes of another. As human beings, we make sense of the world by projecting our thoughts and emotions onto things. This trait serves us well in most endeavors, but it is useless and dangerously misleading when trying to understand the life and message of a man like Jesus.

Men like Jesus and Buddha are not simple extensions of human personalities whose lives can be studied from a distance, without overcoming our individual fears and prejudices. Unless we are willing to dissolve the ignorance that is at the root of our being, we cannot even begin to know them. Jesus says, "Being near me is like being near fire." The light to see the truth comes from burning the wax of ignorance. The deeper the desire to melt, the brighter the light and the greater the understanding. Jesus has been misunderstood not just by the Jews, but also by humanity; we have yet to learn to understand without projecting our own thoughts and emotions.

Self-realized beings are rare expressions of truth, falling into a category of their own. They reveal their secrets only to those who are willing to search within themselves. The easiest way to miss such individuals is by placing them on an unreachable pedestal, projecting our own fears and insecurities onto them. Perhaps this is why it's easier to venerate and worship a man of extraordinary wisdom than to understand him.

Born a Jew, and having peered into the depths of his own psyche, Jesus knew this human weakness all too well. While he was alive, he guarded himself against this age-old problem by often drawing people's attention to his ordinary human nature. Regardless of his seemingly other-worldly appearance and manner, Jesus never let his disciples or the crowds gathered around him forget the fact that he was very much one of their own. However, on that fateful day when he was unjustly tortured and executed, everything changed.

LOST IN TIME

From the moment he was condemned to death, the image of Jesus, subject to a flood of human emotions, began to acquire a different personality, altogether removed from his simple, earthly existence. Over time, the Jesus story, expanding on the turbulent waves of people's untethered passions, swelled large enough to submerge and drown his true human identity.

In just a matter of a few decades, the historical Jesus, the man and the mystic, was lost somewhere in the entangled web of human imaginations, only to be replaced by a wholly mythical figure born out of some of the most glorified interpretations of his life and death.

If one wonders how over two billion Christians have come to believe in the idea of the "Son of God" sent to save them, the simple answer is that, for at least one group of Jews that was trying to make sense of Jesus' life immediately after his death, this idea wasn't so far-fetched after all. When these early believers peered into that colossal crater carved into their souls by the impact of Jesus' gruesome death, they could not help but flood its empty chambers with their most revered beliefs.

In the story of Jesus, the Jews saw their battered and bruised lives - their desperate longing for justice and their unfulfilled prophecy. Unable to see beyond their own self-reflections, they missed the real Jesus altogether. When presented with a map revealing the secrets of a great treasure, one can either choose to explore its hidden mysteries or reverently frame it to be hung on a wall; the Jews of Jerusalem chose the latter.

Fate had provided them with an opportunity to understand and internalize the teachings of Jesus, but instead, they chose to worship him. In their confusion, they threw out the treasure and held on to the chest that once guarded it. As far as these early followers of Jesus were concerned, he was their savior sent by God. No other story about Jesus, real or imaginary, would ever shake their belief in such an idea, for it was not they who had consciously chosen this belief. In its desperate need for survival, this thousand-year-old biblical idea had clung to them for support during one of its most vulnerable hours.

We record, preserve and pass along knowledge from our past that we collectively refer to as our history. If not for this unique human habit, we would still be wandering in the wilderness of life like any other animal, without a sense of purpose or direction. And yet, how often do we seriously question the validity of historical information passed down to us through generations, especially when it is being transmitted through such a flimsy and faulty medium as the human mind?

We rarely acknowledge the tremendous influence our pre-conditioned minds exert on history. We often think of history as a museum housing the relics of our past, where we can simply stroll in at our time of choosing and admire its frozen facts unaffectedly. The word "history," while innocently suggesting that it occupies a quiet space somewhere far away in our distant past, is continuously being rewritten by the present. As fluid as molten rock and as malleable as wet clay, history meanders along like a living and breathing stream, continually lending itself to be shaped and reshaped by our every attempt at trying to grasp it.

There is no such thing as passive observation of history. Whether we like it or not, at the very moment of perceiving history, we also irreversibly alter it by projecting our own thoughts and emotions onto it. While there is hardly a part of history that hasn't been affected by this obvious perceptual barrier, no other story has been so entirely shaped by the limitations of the human mind as the "Son of God" story of Jesus: arguably, one of the greatest myths to ever tumble out of the closet of time.

History is not a recording of facts, but rather an interpretation of them. For over two millennia, human history has been dominated by one popular interpretation of Jesus' life, born out of half-baked spiritual ideas churning within the crucible of religious imagination. The story of a "Son of God" sent to save, especially them, had to make perfect sense to the Jews, for they were already too exhausted to spend any more time and energy understanding a self-realized man's new interpretation of their old beliefs.

Born and raised within the thick walls of prophetic tradition, the Jews had worn the idea of "the chosen ones" on their backs like a second skin. Despite the fragmented state of this idea now, they still couldn't imagine a life devoid of its familiar warmth.

Like many other religions, Judaism had also built its foundation on the shaky grounds of misinterpreted teachings of a few remarkable men of wisdom. Judaism's ever-widening need for control had gradually transformed the simple, insightful spiritual verses of these Jewish mystics into immutable commandments etched in stone. Their over-exaggerated, divinized life stories became central pillars of its faith, drawing people by the millions.

The early followers of Jesus, who had grown fully accustomed to these subtle religious fetters, had no trouble accepting a suitably reimagined Jesus as their savior, as long as they didn't have to sacrifice what they regarded as their fundamental right to be bound to an idea. The central tenet and belief system of Christianity is easiest to understand when we look at it as a hybridized form of Judaism, differing from its traditional parent only in its unconditional acceptance of Jesus as the savior.

We have insisted, without any shred of evidence, that a man who can walk on water and ascend to heaven is somehow rooted in reality. While the Church has done everything in its power to convince us that the "Son of God" story of Jesus is his only story, the real Jesus, the man who walked the earth in flesh and blood, who lived and died urging people to turn inward for their answers, still hides behind that bulwark of human perceptual limitation: Man's inability to see beyond his prejudiced thoughts and emotions - the very same flaw that compelled the Jews of Jerusalem to misunderstand Jesus, the Romans to crucify him, and the Christians to worship him.

The single biggest obstacle that has stood between us and our understanding of Jesus is, unquestionably, that episode of his crucifixion in the hands of the Romans; a grim and grisly event of monumental significance, without which there would be no such thing as Christianity.

Jesus' crucifixion has, all along, been a perfect double-edged sword. On one hand, it drew people to his larger-than-life suffering image, and on the other, it alienated them from his real human story. Thanks to the seismic impact of crucifixion, what should have been a forgettable final chapter of Jesus' life eventually became the central plot around which his entire story revolved. Crucifixion skewed Jesus' image to such an extent that it became almost impossible for people to tell the difference between searching for Jesus and searching for that one extraordinary reason that could convincingly explain why an innocent young man, full of life and light, had to be tortured and killed.

From the emotionally laden depths of human imagination emerged myriad interpretations of Jesus' life, all revolving around the central idea of crucifixion. While most of these expositions were religious in nature, one non-religious interpretation, in particular, is worth reflecting on. Despite appearing to be firmly rooted in facts and history, it still manages to stumble and fall flat on its face.

According to this over-simplified theory that has remained surprisingly popular among the non-believers, Jesus, far from being the "Son of God" sent to save humanity, was a zealot - the leader of an armed radical Jewish militia dedicated to the cause of overthrowing the Romans from Judea. Apparently, this revolutionary Jesus had marched into Jerusalem, along with his army of twelve followers, to rile up the masses against the Roman Empire. Unfortunately for him, this did not unfold as expected, ending in his capture and crucifixion under the Roman charges of sedition.

The fact that some of Jesus' disciples, like Simon and Judas, were known zealots might have given some credence to this theory, but the real bite behind this idea is obvious to see. By putting Jesus in direct conflict with the Romans, this interpretation offers an unambiguous motive for his crucifixion without any necessity to bring God or his divine plans into the picture. It strips the religious armor surrounding Jesus to give us a bare-bones human figure in the middle of an ordinary socio-political struggle.

This uncomplicated image of Jesus would have appealed to many non-believers who were looking for an alternative to the miraculous, "Son of God" theory. However, the inherent flaw of this interpretation is glaringly obvious. In an attempt to steer as far away as possible from the religious image of Jesus, this theory altogether ignores his incredible teachings, drawing a myopic conclusion about his life based solely on crucifixion, as if to proclaim that Jesus' greatest accomplishment was his gruesome death. To call Jesus an armed revolutionary is to miss the mark of understanding by so much that we might as well accept another alternate theory claiming that he was a visiting alien from the planet Nazareth.

Challenging and overthrowing the Roman Empire was probably the last thing on the minds of Jesus and his followers visiting Jerusalem. If they had any such intentions, one would assume that they would have brought along with them some of their homemade weapons of mass destruction - perhaps some oars, hooks, and nets. After all, they were ferocious fishermen from the Sea of Galilee, adept at the art of killing.

As much as we would like to imagine a revolutionary Jesus openly defying a mighty empire, in all probability, he knew nothing about the Romans or their occupation of Jerusalem. In roughly three years of well-documented teachings, Jesus had absolutely nothing to say about the Romans, except once, when he is reported to have said, "Give unto Caesar what belongs to Caesar, and give to God what belongs to God." However, it is unlikely that these are his words. Like so many other Bible verses attributed to Jesus, this might just be a later addition to gain his approval for one other worldly business of man: tax collection.

By the sheer difference in their scale of operation, Jesus and the Romans had to be oblivious to each other's presence. The question, "Did the Romans crucify Jesus because they somehow perceived him as a threat to their rule in Judea?" simply doesn't arise. The very idea that Jesus could even be considered a formidable adversary to the Romans, capable of threatening them, stems entirely from centuries of exaggeration of his image.

The dramatization of Jesus' story made it possible for people to imagine him standing toe-to-toe with the Romans when, in fact, he was so insignificant that they squashed him like a bug. There is no doubting the fact that Jesus was crucified because he posed a threat. The only important question is, to whom?

The Jesus clan was in Jerusalem to address the large congregation of Jews gathered there to celebrate Passover. It was for the sake of these pious and religious Jews that Jesus had made this long trip. He had come to Jerusalem to share his newfound realization - to offer his people a radical spiritual possibility that could liberate them from their daily strife and struggle. Being one of their own, he was hoping that they would embrace his message with little resistance. However, it did not take him long to realize that to have any chance of success, he had to first break through a seemingly insurmountable obstacle: the time-hardened brick wall of Jewish orthodoxy.

As a realized man, Jesus was able to clearly see all that had gone wrong within Jewish society. By mis-understanding their past, they had given in to needless fear and worry, turning their ancestral religion into a sacrificial ritual, which included the slaughtering of animals and burning them on the altar to please their God.

This Jewish interpretation of sacrifice, known as "Korban", eventually became the central religious tenet shaping both Christianity and Islam. Jesus expressed his disdain for such meaningless traditions in as clear a fashion as he could when he whipped the moneylenders outside the temple and overturned their tables.

In challenging Jewish orthodoxy, Jesus was questioning not just the religious beliefs of the Jews, but also their way of life. Unlike many modern-day religions, Judaism was not a Sunday sect. Religion penetrated every single aspect of daily Jewish life. By ridiculing their sacredly held ancient traditions, Jesus was gnawing at the very root of Jewish existence.

Not surprisingly, the Jewish priests saw him as an immediate threat to their authority. One among them, Joseph ben Caiaphas, took it upon himself personally to see to it that this Jesus nuisance was dealt with at once. It was under his direction that Jesus was captured and tried by the Jewish Sanhedrin, where he was accused of several religious crimes, including threatening to destroy the Jewish temple and calling himself "King of the Jews." Although it was the

Roman sword that severed Jesus' life from his body, the hand wielding that sword had all along been that of an insecure Jewish priest.

BETWEEN A ROCK AND A HARD PLACE

Jerusalem's rapidly changing political and religious landscape had pushed the Jews to the brink of chaotic disintegration. The arrival of Jesus, and more importantly, his grisly execution, only plunged them even further into chaos.

In less than a century after Jesus' death, the Jews had fallen from the exalted pedestal of God's chosen ones to being derided as traitors. Their homeland was besieged, the temple destroyed, and they were robbed of all that was precious and sacred to them, reducing them to living like outsiders in their own backyard. It seemed as though fate had at last caught up with the weathered and beaten Jewish spirits, stripping them of all their choices except one - to decide how they wished to relinquish their religious supremacy; in a rebellion, kicking and screaming, or quietly unan-nounced.

Either way, squeezed between the mighty Roman Empire and a fast-growing Jesus movement, the traditional Jewish way of life was slowly but surely being pushed toward the edge of the cliff of time. What Jesus tried to accomplish in life, he seemed to be getting done in his death. Internal dissension over Jesus' life, his message, and his crucifixion, were ripping apart the carefully interwoven fabric of Jewish society. Of all the forces capable of threatening the Jews, their biggest nemesis turned out to be one of their very own.

But Jesus, like many teachers who had come before him in the hopes of shaking up the established religious system of the Jews, totally underestimated their resilience in holding on to their familiar way of life. He had forgotten that the biggest strength of the Jews was neither Jerusalem nor their faith. Rather, it was that indomitable Jewish spirit forged inside Jerusalem's furnace of human conflicts and toughened by centuries of relentlessly defending their faith.

If there was ever a race of people capable of handling such overwhelming religious, political, and moral assaults to escape certain extermination, it had to be the Jews. Even with all his wisdom and intelligence, Jesus could not have imagined that from the rubble of their crumbling past, the Jews would rebuild a new religious empire around his broken body.

The threat of extermination was nothing new to the Jews. They had been fighting annihilation practically their entire lives. As no strangers to religious and political upheavals, the Jews had always found ways of dealing with their never-ending list of predicaments. Jesus was one more obstacle standing in their way, although he was their biggest trial yet.

Jesus posed an unusual challenge to the Jews, threatening their existence either way, whether they embraced him or not. He presented them with two equally frightful choices: accepting him in his entirety meant willfully erasing their religious past, and rejecting him meant risking being branded as traitors for life. While they somehow managed to do away with the physical threat of Jesus by getting rid of him as quickly as possible, there was no straightforward answer to dealing with his rapidly expanding image, which was a direct result of their imprudent handling of him.

The Jews were pinned to the wall by two mighty forces: the Roman Empire and the rising Jesus movement, both showing utter contempt for the Jewish way of life and hell-bent on bringing it down. Stuck between a rock and a hard place, they pulled out one of the oldest tricks from their biblical book of survival - a strategy that had served them well every time their way of life was under threat by a new individual expression of Truth.

In fact, over the centuries, the Jewish Bible had become a perfect playbook for identifying and getting rid of any newly emerging sapling of individuality. Clearly spelled out in their religious scriptures and deeply embedded in their psyche, the perfect solution to the Jesus problem had always been a part of the collective consciousness of the Jews. They had played this religious game for far too long to fail at it now.

In a classic case of religious sophistry, the Jews solved the Jesus riddle by both accepting and rejecting him at the same time. While openly embracing Jesus' outermost name and form, they quietly hollowed out his rebellious insides and filled them with their own biblical stories, ensuring the continuity of their beliefs inside a newly sanctified Jesus crucible called Christianity.

Jesus might have been a stranger to the ways and habits of Jerusalem, but even stranger was Jerusalem to Jesus' naked, unpolished, and fearless individuality. Amidst a sea of followers and undulating figments of social imagination, Jesus was a free man - untethered, undivided, and complete - the very definition of the word "individual."

It was to this sacred inner space Jesus was referring when he said, "The kingdom of heaven is within you; return." Jesus' kingdom is not some esoteric, out-of-this-world, imaginary place open only to a select few. It has always been that simple truth hidden within each and every individual, available to all those who are willing to seek it, be they a sinner or saint, believer or nonbeliever, rock star or recluse.

Jesus' message was for all, and it was extraordinarily simple. He was urging his fellow human beings to awaken to their original state of being, to find refuge in their pure inner stillness, far away from the ever-changing world of dreams and desires, and to become fully alive, fully awake, and fully human again. He was saying the exact same thing Buddha had said five centuries before him. When asked if he was a man or a god, Buddha had replied, "I am neither. I am just awake while you are all still asleep."

The Jews of Jerusalem misunderstood Jesus and over-exaggerated his abilities only because they had become total strangers to the phenomenon of individuality. They had been too preoccupied fighting common enemies and struggling to preserve their collective identity to explore the vast depths and possibilities of individuality.

The same insightful words of Jesus that make perfect sense when heard during moments of peace and stability had the opposite effect in a chaotic, war-torn Jerusalem. Jesus could not have chosen a more inappropriate place, audience, or season to share his radical spiritual message. His rebellious tone and choice of words were a dead giveaway that he was totally oblivious to the precarious position the Jews of Jerusalem were in. Addressing a disturbed bunch of people who were desperately searching for some sense of peace and stability, he told them, "I have come not to bring peace but the sword."

In a way, Jesus was offering the Jews the very same thing they were trying to run away from. While they were looking for ways to ward off the bitter cold of violence and injustice, he was telling them to take off their clothes and trample them under their feet. It's no surprise that Jesus' revolutionary words fell on the Jewish spirit like salt sprinkled on a raw, gaping wound. Eventually, Jerusalem treated Jesus as it would someone trying to snatch away its warm, cozy blanket in the dead of winter.

Both Islam and Buddhism became major world religions partly because their religious teachers lived long enough to establish their teachings and ways of life in society. Muhammad was in his sixties when he died, and Buddha was almost eighty. Jesus had only been teaching for a few years before he was crucified in his early thirties, so he didn't have enough time to firmly establish his teachings among the people.

Young Jesus had around twelve disciples with him, most of whom had hardly grasped his message of internal self-realization. They were waiting for him to bring the "Kingdom of Heaven" down to earth, and when he was crucified, they were devastated. They thought they had been fooled into believing in a false messiah. They had lost all trust in his words and didn't want any part of him.

Jesus' Christianity died on the cross. So how did his story and message re-emerge from the dead and take root in the hearts and minds of the people, to become a major religious movement? Who resurrected Jesus and his teachings? What happened during those three days between Jesus' death and his so-called resurrection? More importantly, who was that woman who was the first witness to his "resurrection?"

The Greatest Love Story Never Told

FALLING IN LOVE

Mary Magdalene is a figure shrouded in mystery. Scripturally, there is very little that has survived about her, mainly because she represented the single biggest evidence that Jesus was a man. Over the centuries, the Church has done everything in its power to vilify Mary Magdalene's name, distance her from Jesus, and discredit her story and the extraordinary influence she had on the Jesus movement. The Gnostic Gospels, written by Jesus' closest disciples and rejected at the council of Nicaea, however, reveal a much more powerful, influential, and intimate Mary Magdalene.

The Jewish culture prohibited women from studying religious scriptures and pursuing a spiritual way of life. As a learned woman interested in exploring the hidden mysteries of life, Miriam from Magdala was an outcast from the beginning. In the eyes of the Jews, she was a fallen woman. Mary fell in love with Jesus' simplicity, words, and manners, and decided to leave behind Magdala and everything familiar to follow him.

Mary's thirst for truth is what attracted her to Jesus in the first place. She was searching for the purpose of life and had found her answer in Jesus' message. She falls in love with Jesus and all that he represented to become his favorite disciple and devoted companion, supporting him in every way possible.

Mary Magdalene tended to all of Jesus' physical needs, including arranging for his travels, keeping a detailed record of his teachings, and even guiding the disciples on his behalf. She became an inseparable part of Jesus' life, assuming the roles of his wife, sister, and mother, to become his only family.

In the Gnostic Gospels, Mary Magdalene is not only referred to as the "apostle of apostles," but also as Jesus' companion, whom he often kissed on the mouth - in other words, his wife. There is enough evidence to suggest that Jesus was married - the most important being - if he weren't, it would have been impossible for him to teach in the synagogues. The Jewish tradition regarded unmarried men as incomplete and hence unfit to teach. To be referred to as a rabbi, Jesus had to be married.

For many of us, it's hard to picture a married Jesus. We have come to accept such a dry-cleaned image of him, stripped of all his human frailties, that it is difficult to even conceive of such a possibility, although many of Jesus' disciples, including Simon Peter, Judas Iscariot, Philip, Andrew, and Bartholomew, were all married. Marriage was such an integral part of Jewish society that those who chose to remain single, like John and James, are singled out in the Bible to be referred to as lifelong virgins, just to emphasize the fact that they were unmarried. It is hard to imagine why, for no apparent reason, Jesus would be an exception to this rule.

While the Bible has been ready to draw our attention to this unusual status as if it were a badge of honor, it never once refers to Jesus as a virgin - a point if indeed true, would have probably been reiterated at least a dozen times. After all, what better way to say that Jesus was not an ordinary human being than by emphasizing the fact that he was a lifelong virgin who had dedicated himself to the service of God?

To a spiritual woman like Mary, Jesus represented the totality of what she was seeking. To be in love with a man like him and to be an integral part of his life meant everything to her. Mary was intimate with Jesus in every sense of the term. She might have given birth before, but she was certainly pregnant when Jesus was sentenced to be crucified.

Mary Magdalene and Jesus' intimacy did not end at the physical or emotional level. They were most intimate with each other in moments of spiritual reflection. The conversations between them went much beyond the daily routine of life - they dove into the inner mysteries of life together. With Jesus personally guiding her along the way, Mary had greatly progressed on the spiritual path and was ripe for her own realization.

Living with Jesus, reflecting on his teachings, and caring for and loving him had become Mary's entire life. She was blissfully unaware of how inseparably intertwined her life had become with that of Jesus - she came to a full realization of this fact the day he was crucified.

For many who were there to watch the show, Jesus was just another rebel who deserved to be punished. For bystanders, he was simply another face. To a handful of disciples, he was their teacher. But for Mary Magdalene, he was everything.

Suffering is a direct consequence of how deeply we are attached to the thing we are about to lose. The purpose of a spiritual quest is to learn the art of seeing our own mind and body with a sense of detachment. If attachment is the root of all suffering, then learning how to stay detached is the way out of it.

As a fully realized man, Jesus had already transcended the psychological and emotional attachment to his body. During the crucifixion he could feel the immense physical pain in his body, but he was numb to the emotional pain associated with the thought of dying. He quietly endured the pain of crucifixion, hardly uttering a word throughout the ordeal.

For Mary, though, it was an entirely different matter. Mary Magdalene's attachment to Jesus was total; hence, her suffering was absolute. In fact, it would be perfectly alright to say that during Jesus' crucifixion, Mary suffered more than Jesus himself. For her, the pain didn't stop at the physical level. It flowed like molten iron into her mind, body, and spirit, making its way into every pore of her being. With every blow, the Roman whip was tearing into his flesh and her memories at the same time.

Amidst the noise of jeering crowds, Mary watched the all-too-familiar glistening skin of the Jesus she had cared for, caressed, and kissed, rip apart and spill its horrors. Every scourge upon his body was a scar on her soul. She watched helplessly as ignorance mockingly tore into the flesh of her truth. She watched as her love was being drained out of his body. She watched as the guiding light of her life faded and disappeared forever. Mary did not suffer that day - she died on the cross with Jesus. Everything familiar to her vanished that day.

The brutality of Roman crucifixion didn't end with the death of its unfortunate victim - its horrors continued. Victims of crucifixion rarely received a proper burial. They were left on the cross as display, sometimes for weeks, as they decomposed in full view of the general public. What remained of these half-decomposed bodies was thrown into a common pit to be gathered by their mourning relatives.

While the Bible gives us a dignified account of Jesus' burial, it is more than likely that he received the same Roman treatment as any other crucified Jew. Mary's blood-curdling screams of anguish did not end with Jesus' death - her ordeal had only begun.

As the crowd gathered there retreated and Jesus' disciples stayed away out of fear of persecution, Mary and her broken heart were the only companions around Jesus. The image of pregnant Mary alone at the foot of the cross, guarding her husband's broken body, seared into people's memory to become an indelible symbol of human suffering.

Christians believe that three days after his crucifixion, Jesus came back to life and bodily ascended to heaven. Whether it was three days or more, something did happen between Jesus' death and his "resurrection" - a period of monumental significance upon which rests the foundation of the world's largest faith.

The Bible acknowledges that Mary Magdalene was the first witness to Jesus' resurrection, but it misses the point that resurrection wasn't an objective physical experience that happened in the outer world for all to witness. Instead, it was a subjective inner spiritual experience of a devoted disciple who, in her moment of absolute desperation, realized the totality of her master's teachings within her. Mary Magdalene wasn't just the first witness to Jesus' "resurrection" - she was the only witness to it.

Drawing from other similar transcendental experiences, the nature of Jesus and Mary's relationship, and our own intuitive imagination, we can piece together what might have happened during those few days between Jesus' death and his so-called resurrection.

While everything she knew as her life hung on the cross, Mary had nowhere to go. As she sits at Jesus' feet, the same feet she had so often washed, perfumed, and kissed, she stares at his lifeless body, desperately searching for any sign of life behind his deep sunken eyes, unaware that the spirit that had so beautifully adorned the earthly body of Jesus had already deserted him. Her Yeshua was just another body now, waiting to be devoured by time.

Having exhausted all her tears, Mary is beyond grief - and yet, she isn't anywhere near letting go of Jesus; she doesn't even know what that means. She sits there, in the middle of nowhere, having lost everything, reflecting on the life that once was. As pain blurs her surroundings, widening the gap between her mind and body, the physicality of her life gives way to her memories of Jesus. While her body is fully aware of what has just happened, her mind is unwilling to accept reality, circling back to the thought that there is something she is missing.

Perhaps he isn't really gone but is only trying to teach her something she is unable to get. Amidst an unrelenting flood of confusing thoughts, memories, and emotions, she begins to hear him. Jesus' words and teachings rush into Mary's memory. She remembers the time she had asked him about the nature of his reality, and he had replied that he is the undivided life dwelling within everything, including her.

Hope shoots through Mary's veins when she realizes that she cannot lose her Jesus, for he is within her. She remembers his words, "Seek and you shall find," and desperately begins to search. She searches through every nook and cranny of her mind, and all she can find are his memories, stemming from her hopeless longing.

However, in her years of dedicated spiritual seeking, Mary had wandered the wastelands of her mind too much to not know the difference between what she is seeking and what she is imagining. This was the difference between Mary Magdalene and any other disciple of Jesus: she was adept at the art of searching, and could not easily be fooled by her mind. The art of watching that Jesus had taught her had not abandoned her, even in this hour of absolute desperation.

For the next few days, Mary moves in and out of her mind, desperately trying to find her Jesus. She searches through his words and silence - through her memories and imagination. She searches with her eyes closed and open, in moments of stillness and in moments of rage.

She calls for him like a mother, longs for him like a lover, and begs for him like a child.

At the end of it all, Mary is utterly exhausted - too weak to even think or imagine. She is on the verge of giving up her search and her life, but her undying desire to meet Jesus keeps her alive and awake. When she has no more thoughts in her mind, when she has exhausted all her options of finding him, when she finally surrenders her search - it happens. In her moment of absolute internal silence and stillness, Mary quietly slips into another realm of reality to witness what she had been searching for all her life.

Mary is in a place of unimaginable bliss and grandeur. Her pain and anguish are gone. She can no longer smell the stench of rotting bodies or hear the wailing of wild beasts. She can no longer feel the weight of her exhausted body or its aching pain. Her familiar life has disappeared from her consciousness to give way to a new reality beyond everything she knows - beyond images and experiences, people and places, time and space. She is in an enlightened realm - a formless, shapeless, limitless expanse of aliveness.

Mary Magdalene was in her moment of Nirvana - what the Buddha called "Nothingness." She had, at last, found Jesus' "Eternal Life," to understand the true meaning of his teachings. In that moment of transcendental ecstasy, Mary had become a silent witness to Jesus' life and message. Through her love, longing, and realization, Mary Magdalene had resurrected Jesus from the dead, affirming the eternal nature of his being and the truth of his teachings. She had, at last, attained her life's purpose: to be a witness to Jesus' truth.

Without her knowledge, Mary Magdalene had been preparing herself for this moment her whole life. This is why she became interested in a spiritual way of life, was drawn to Jesus, and spent all those years studying under him - why she refused to submit to unfair rules set by man for her, and why she chose not to hide her beautiful golden brown hair under a religious garb, despite being ridiculed and cast out.

Mary's life was a preparation to internalize Jesus's teachings - to become a womb for his virgin birth. If life makes sense only backward when seen from the vantage point of an extraordinary event, then what happened to Mary after Jesus' crucifixion almost entirely defines her. It was Mary's destiny to pour her whole being into Jesus, and when he is taken away from her, fall back to the source - her original state of being. Mary had become a living embodiment of Jesus' words, "Return, the kingdom of heaven is within you."

The lives of Jesus and Mary are incomplete without each other. Without Mary, Jesus would have disappeared, leaving no mark on the pages of history, and without Jesus, Mary would have never attained her life's purpose. All their lives, they gravitated toward each other to become complete. Jesus became the perfect object of Mary's love, and Mary became the emptiness that received his truth. Amidst all the insults, trials, and tribulations, their love had triumphed. In the truest sense, they had become one. The world has yet to witness a better love story.

Holding Jesus' broken body in her lap, hiding his earthly seed in her womb, and bearing the truth of his teachings in her heart, Mary becomes the very definition of the word "mother." She gathers Jesus' distraught disciples, consoles them, and urges them not to mourn. She tells them that Jesus isn't dead - he is alive in her, in them, and in everything else. He is the imperishable eternal life whose every word has come true in her - she has seen him.

It is Mary's words that eventually become the foundation of the Jesus movement. Mary Magdalene is the missing link between Jesus and his faith - there is no Christianity without Mary and her internalization of Jesus' truth. If Mary Magdalene had been a man, in all likelihood, her Christianity would have replaced that of Jesus'. Despite her being a woman and living in a society dominated by men, even to this day, it is her story of Jesus that the world is most familiar with.

By virtue of her unconditional devotion to Jesus and his cause, Mary Magdalene had raised herself to the status of "mother." There is no other title more befitting her that can encompass the totality of what she represented. Mary loved and cared for Jesus like a mother, gave a virgin birth to his life and movement, and just like a mother, healed the broken hearts of his disciples and guided them in the right direction.

For the next few years following Jesus' death, Mary manages to accomplish something even Jesus himself was unable to. Unknowingly, by the sheer strength of her conviction in Jesus' message, she lays the necessary groundwork for the dissemination of his teachings. She provides the most needed emotional narrative that binds the Jesus story to the hearts and minds of the people. As an endearing symbol of love, wisdom, and strength, for the early Christians, she becomes their beloved "Mother Mary." As a tribute to her motherhood, the fitting image of young Mary with her newborn child, becomes an inseparable part of the Christian imagination.

SILENCED

While the Bible has dismissed Mary Magdalene as a repentant sinner who was once saved by Jesus, the Gnostic Gospels give us a more wholesome image of her, including the complex relationship she shared with the other disciples and the extent to which she influenced the Jesus movement.

Here, far from being a sinner bewitched by demons, Mary Magdalene is a woman of extraordinary intelligence and importance. She possesses a deep understanding of the spiritual teachings of Jesus, and is often the one to guide the disciples in his absence. She is also usually the first one to ask questions and lead the discussions. Mary Magdalene is recognized as Jesus' closest disciple, whom he loved and trusted.

The Gospel of Mary Magdalene reveals that some of the disciples were jealous of Mary's intelligence, popularity, and closeness to Jesus - particularly Peter who, in one instance, even asks that she be removed from the discussions. Simon Peter was known to be stubborn and hardheaded. Very little of Jesus' subtle teachings entered his thick masculine skull. He was waiting for the arrival of a literal, physical kingdom of God where Jesus would sit on a throne like a king and rule. For this reason, Jesus aptly referred to him as "a rock" - an epithet that was mistaken for a compliment.

There is one intriguing passage in the Gnostic Gospels that beautifully captures Mary Magdalene's true place in Jesus' life, and the complex relationship she shared with the rest of the group. The disciples ask her to speak about some secret teachings Jesus had shared only with her, of which none of them were aware. They reasoned that Jesus loved Mary more than any other woman, so surely he must have shared something profound with her.

Mary agrees and talks about the nature of reality and her experience of realizing Jesus' truth within herself. While some of the disciples question the depth of her insight and the strangeness of her experience, Peter outright rejects her experience, saying, "How could the master have spoken such things privately to a woman and not to us?"

Hurt by this rejection, Mary weeps and asks Peter how he could think that she is just making all this up. Levi intervenes to say, "Peter, you have always been hot-tempered. If Jesus considered her worthy, who are you indeed to reject her? Surely, he knew her very well. He loved her more than us."

The Gnostic Gospels also inform us that Mary had her own independent realization of Truth. Jesus had revealed to her the most intimate secrets of life, which she had fully realized within herself After Jesus' crucifixion, it was Mary who consoled the distraught and shaken disciples, giving them the necessary strength to go forth and spread his teachings. After Jesus' death, Mary became both the binding force and the guiding light of the Jesus community.

Mary Magdalene was a fully self-realized, enlightened saint whose interpretation of Jesus' teachings shows, beyond any doubt, that she knew exactly what he was referring to. The profundity of her words can be matched only by that of Jesus.

Her last remark before leaving Judea shows just how deep and profound her understanding of life was: "I left the world with the aid of another world. A design was erased, by virtue of a higher design. Henceforth, I travel toward repose, where time rests in the eternity of time. I go now into silence." These are not the words of a repentant sinner, but of a woman who had realized eternity within herself. Although she is referring to the inner world, ironically, silence became Mary's reality in the outer world as well.

The divinity of Jesus was an unquestionable, immovable cornerstone of the Christian faith, upon which rested the entire purpose of the Church. Mary Magdalene and the truth of her story represented irrefutable evidence that Jesus was an ordinary man - that he was birthed, lived, and died just like any other mortal human being.

By threatening to bring Jesus down from the high heavens to the level of ordinary human under-standing, Mary Magdalene was presenting an insurmountable obstacle to the Church. To accept Mary's truth would have meant unconditionally accepting the truth of Jesus' life - that he was not the "Son of God," but one of our very own. Mary Magdalene was branded a sinner and a prostitute only because she refused to snugly fit inside Catholic doctrine. Her truth had no place amidst the miraculous "Son of God" narrative of Jesus.

Sooner or later, the Church had to officially recognize Mary's faith. As one of the most important figures of the Jesus movement, as Jesus' wife, closest disciple, and the Mother of the Church, Mary Magdalene had become an inseparable part of the living faith of the Jesus community. By the fourth century AD, she had become too big a phenomenon to be simply brushed aside. Catholic Christianity eventually accepted Mary's faith, but not before committing one of the most atrocious crimes imaginable.

In 431 AD, at the council of Ephesus, in one of the most grotesque theological plays on words, Mary was officially recognized as "Theotokos," or "Mother of God." With a single swipe of its talons, the Church had scooped up Mary Magdalene's magnificent life and deposited it into its theological nest of half-incubated ideas.

Mary Magdalene revered as the Mother of the Church

From this moment onward, Christians would always know Mary Magdalene as someone she never was: revered and worshiped as Jesus' mother, and despised as a prostitute and a sinner. The sheer brilliance and subtlety of this manipulation to hide Jesus' true identity remains, to this day, one of the greatest cover-ups in human history. Nowhere else has the power of organized religion been displayed with such crafty insensitivity.

No one knows the names of Jesus' parents or who they actually were. Jesus' birth stories in the Bible were later additions inserted to complete his savior narrative. There is a difference in how history remembers the lives of ordinary men and those who have awakened to their highest nature. A spiritual man's life enters history books only after they begin to teach. Everything we know about such a person comes exclusively from the memory of their students. The story of Jesus wasn't recorded by historians, but by a handful of his closest disciples, who couldn't have cared any less about his mother and father.

Jesus had left home so early that it is more than likely he would have forgotten all about his parents. Besides, Jesus himself made it abundantly clear that he was against all family ties that bind one to the past. As an enlightened individual trying to awaken others from their deep slumber of life, Jesus would have known all too well that the single biggest obstacle to awakening is attachment to one's earthly roots.

There is no ambiguity in Jesus' response when he is asked who his mother and brothers were. Pointing to the disciples he says, "Here are my mother and my brothers. Whoever does the will of my Father is my brother, sister, and mother." In another instance, he says, "He who knows the father and the mother will be called the son of a harlot. Whoever does not hate his father and his mother cannot become a disciple of mine, and whoever does not hate his brothers and sisters will not be worthy of me."

Jesus was a spiritual man totally cut off from traditional family life. Everything we know about him is a reflection of how his disciples saw and remembered him, with no place for any mother and father sentiments. The reason why we know nothing about Jesus' parents is the same reason why we have not bothered to ask who the mothers and fathers of Buddha, Muhammad, and Abraham were. It's a detail that is irrelevant to their stories.

There is no precedent in history of a prophet's mother being worshiped. Catholic Christianity has entirely deviated from this norm in choosing to venerate and worship "Jesus' mother." In the Catholic tradition, Mary is as important a figure as Jesus. In fact, the worship tradition of Mary predates that of Jesus. Some of the earliest Christian churches were dedicated not to Jesus, but to Mary. Outsiders have always wondered about the strangeness of this Catholic tradition, unaware of the fact that it isn't Jesus' mother who is being worshiped, but his wife, whose broken heart was the birthplace of Christianity.

For the past 1500 years, we have been worshiping an imaginary Mother of Jesus who was never a part of history. The images, rituals, and symbolisms of Mary, the supposed Mother of Jesus, all belong to that one woman who was an inseparable part of Jesus' life - his wife, Mary Magdalene.

The single biggest evidence giving away Mary's true identity hides in plain sight, in her unique representation in religious art. We have never bothered to ask why Mother Mary is always represented as a young woman. If she was indeed the mother of Jesus, then, in all likelihood, she would have been depicted as a much older woman, standing either alone or beside Jesus. There isn't a single Christian church in the world representing Mary as an older woman - a fact that simply cannot be brushed aside as incidental.

Religious art and its symbolisms capturing human stories do not emerge from imagination; they draw their roots from the memories of people. Although time distorts and exaggerates human representation in art, its inspiration can always be traced back to an original source rooted in reality.

It is highly unlikely for the most popular Christian image of Mary, holding "baby Jesus" in her arms, to have come from a source rooted in reality, for the simple reason that, growing up, Jesus was just another ordinary child. There is no reason why anybody should have cared to remember baby Jesus or his mother. It is impossible for this image to have come from the memory of people - unless, of course, it is an image of an entirely different woman whose extraordinary life and story just had to be remembered.

In religious art, Mary is depicted as a younger woman simply because that is how people remembered her - she wasn't the mother of Jesus but his wife. The infant in her arms isn't Jesus but his child. The crown of twelve stars representing the twelve apostles of Jesus, the bleeding heart symbolizing her suffering, and the lily flower personifying her purity, are all symbolisms adorning the immaculate spirit of Mary Magdalene who was revered as the apostle of apostles, Jesus' favorite disciple, and the Mother of the Church.

For centuries, we have been worshiping an imaginary mother who was never a part of the most important episodes of Jesus' life, while the woman who walked with Jesus until the very end, who fell in love with him and his message, who became a witness to his truth, and without whom we would know nothing about a man named Jesus, is all but erased from human memory.

The story of Mary Magdalene is, in a way, the story of every woman in history. Women have been suppressed, vilified, and persecuted in virtually every male-dominated society, not because of their flaws, but because they are inherently, by nature, emotionally and spiritually stronger than men. History shows that men have always feared the mind of an independent, free-thinking woman whose simple ways, childlike innocence, and earthy, rooted nature made her a formidable spiritual partner, more ripe for realization than man.

An individual's true strength comes not from brute physical force but from a quieter, subtler inner dimension. The softer qualities of simplicity, love, forgiveness, acceptance, and compassion that Jesus was urging men to develop were all essentially feminine qualities. For centuries, women have quietly endured the injustice of a male-dominated society, not because they could not match up to man's strengths or ambitions but simply because they didn't need to.

Spiritually, men and women are the yin and yang of existence - two opposing forces meant to perfectly complement and complete each other. By design, men were created physically strong to deal with the harshness of life, and women emotionally robust to keep things rooted and in perspective. If becoming spiritual is all about going inside to get back to the roots of one's being, then a woman is naturally more adept at navigating the subtle inner realms of life. More than anything else, men have feared this incredible ability of a woman to be perfectly at home within herself, willing to go as deep as it takes to find herself.

Perhaps this is why many ancient, overly masculine cultures prohibited women from studying the scriptures, pursuing a spiritual way of life, and even participating in social life. With none of his physical strengths, ambitious desires, ability to plot, scheme, and organize aiding him in his inner journey, a man would have naturally felt insecure in the presence of a spiritual woman possessing an intuitive understanding of life.

It isn't surprising that of all the people who had gathered around Jesus - those who heard him and those who followed him - it was ultimately a woman who managed to fully understand and internalize his message.

The weak have no need to be subjugated. They submit to authority readily. It is usually the strong who are feared and hence suppressed. The biggest obstacle to a religion's unrestrained outward expansion - its ambitious, politically motivated way of life - has always been the simple, contented, rooted nature of the feminine. Man figured out very early that the only way he can go about spreading his pseudo-religious understanding of life is by keeping the woman and her rebellious spiritual nature suppressed.

From the moment it chose to disregard Jesus' original teachings, which were all about the balance between the male and the female, Christianity resigned itself to being a spiritually closed institution, oblivious to everything feminine. Despite its logical sophistication, the Catholic doctrine could not accommodate a simple love story of a woman and her teacher. Like countless other women in history, Mary Magdalene was a victim of man's fragile ego.

While most male-dominated religions simply sidelined women, a highly organized and centralized Roman Christianity took its bias against women to a whole new level. As an institution utterly devoid of the feminine perspective, its spiritual ignorance would eventually prove to be catastrophic for women.

The Church-sanctioned witch hunts of the fifteen hundreds were easily one of the most barbaric demonstrations of this prejudice against women anywhere, rooted entirely in ignorance. While acting in the name of suppressing heresy, the Church was mercilessly smothering all existing and newly emerging branches of wisdom, blanketing them under its thick sheepskin of biblical theology. In the name of witch hunts, it went about systematically identifying and eliminating all free-thinking, individualistic, and spiritual women.

Between 1400 and 1700 AD, it is estimated that more than a hundred thousand women were executed with the accusation of witchcraft. If you happened to be a woman living in Europe during this period, you could have been branded a witch and burnt alive at the stake if you had more than a couple of female friends, were rich and independent, knew how to swim, or had a mole on your back.

Although they were not persecuted, the condition of women during first-century Jerusalem wasn't any better. By denying her existential right to freedom, Judaism had clipped the wings of the Jewish woman, forcing her to live under the shadows of a deeply prejudiced socio-political structure fashioned by man for himself. One can only imagine the plight of a spiritual woman like Mary Magdalene, who had to fight all her life for her basic right to be recognized as an individual - just to be able to live, love, and breathe in freedom.

Having realized the ultimate truth of Jesus' message within herself, Mary had the daunting task of sharing her realization with others. She had to speak her mind while looking into those suspicious masculine eyes that had already pronounced her guilty just because she was born a woman. Not surprisingly, her truth was met with disbelief, doubt, and mistrust. The disciples questioned the strangeness of Mary's words, the authenticity of her experiences, and the purity of her intentions. But more than anything else, they questioned a woman's authority to speak.

RETREAT TO THE MOUNTAINS

Jesus' death dramatically alters the relationship between Mary Magdalene and the other disciples, especially Peter, who had trouble accepting the fact that Jesus had shared some of the most intimate secrets of life with a woman. The very thought of accepting a woman as his teacher had blocked his ability to see Mary's sincere devotion and love toward the disciples.

While Jesus was alive, Peter could not openly challenge Mary's unique position and her authority to teach. Jesus' love and admiration for Mary were obvious, and he had dared not reject her in his presence. Now that the master was gone, Peter could openly question and challenge the strange ways and manners of this spiritual woman.

By rejecting Mary Magdalene's internal experience of Truth, Peter was rejecting her version of Jesus entirely. This conflict between Mary and Peter is crucial to understanding Christianity, for this is where the early Jesus movement branched off into two opposing ideologies: one born out of Mary Magdalene's internal realization of Jesus' truth, and the other that emerged from Peter's literal interpretation of the "Kingdom of Heaven."

Irrespective of whether the disciples fully understood or agreed with Mary or not, it is certain that after listening to her experience, their understanding of Jesus begins to change. Eventually, it is Mary's conviction in Jesus' words that re-instills the confidence of the distraught disciples, giving them the necessary strength to go forth and spread his teachings.

Mary's deeply emotional and personal story of Jesus quickly caught on like wildfire, and became a new growing spiritual movement. Mary Magdalene's biggest contribution to the Jesus movement was her repose - the silent cry of her bleeding heart is what we now recognize as Christianity. It is her love, anguish, pain, and suffering in one form or another that have resonated in the hallowed chambers of the Christian church for over two millennia.

Despite Mary's best efforts to share her realization, her spiritual interpretation of Jesus' message is met with stoic skepticism and hostility. Soon she finds herself amidst a sea of faces that hate her very presence. Without Jesus to shield her from such animosity, a vulnerable, helpless, and rejected Mary Magdalene decides to retreat - go as far away as possible from everything human.

One cannot be certain if Mary actually chose to leave Judea or if she was, as the stories recount, set sail on a rudderless ship to slowly drift away and perish - although it is highly unlikely that she would have made it all the way from Judea to France on a broken ship with no supplies, her fate left entirely to the mercy of the winds.

In all likelihood, "rudderless ship" was simply a metaphor referring to the fact that without Jesus, Mary was now a "rudderless ship" lost in the high seas of life. Willingly or unwillingly, Mary Magdalene did leave Judea along with Mary Jacobe, Mary Salome, and sister Martha. Also on the boat were several other close followers of Jesus, including Cedonius, Maximin, and Lazarus. Drifting in the Mediterranean for several months, these castaways arrived at the southern coast of France, at a place which is now known as Saintes-Maries-de-la-Mer, "The Three Marys of the Sea."

These original followers of Jesus moved inland to Marseille, one of the oldest cities in France, where they began preaching, sowing the first seeds of the Christian movement in its strange but fertile soil. While Mary's brother Lazarus became the first bishop of Marseille and Maximin the bishop of Aix, Mary Magdalene retreated into a mountain cave to spend the next thirty years of her life in silent contemplation and meditation until her death.

The mountains where she lived are named St. Baume Mountains after her, symbolizing the alabaster jar of perfume she always carried with her - the one she used in anointing Jesus' feet. "Baume" comes from Latin "balsamum", which means "perfume." The grotto where she lived is now a full-scale monastery open to the public, where devotees have been making pilgrimages since the fifth century. Here, beneath an alabaster statue of Mary Magdalene, sits a reliquary housing her bones.

In the nearby medieval town of Saint-Maximin-La-Sainte-Baume, in a basilica dedicated to Mary Magdalene, rests a sealed glass dome containing her skull. It is paraded around the town every year on July 22, her birthday.

In time, Mary Magdalene became one of the most revered saints of France, with her churches scattered all across the land. The perfumed scent of Mary's extraordinary life still lingers in the air of France - a magical place impregnated with the grace, beauty, wisdom, and softness of this sacred feminine.

In a world dominated by men, the art, architecture, and culture of France stood out as a resounding example of effeminate beauty. For almost a thousand years, southern France was renowned for its balanced, progressive thinking - a constant influx of fresh creative ideas that allowed art, music, and literature to flourish. It was a place where women held important positions of power, were treated with unusual respect, and, unlike anywhere else in the world at that time, enjoyed levels of freedom unheard of. France, for a long time, stood out as one of the most beautiful examples of a culture brimming with the female archetype.

The Grotto of Mary Magdalene

By the third century AD, the story of Mary Magdalene and her Jesus had seeped into the hearts and minds of the people, becoming the "Christian Movement." The extraordinary tale of their struggles had trickled down into every possible form of human expression. Jesus and Mary now occupied a central place in some of the world's most beautiful art. Their story and its symbolism were the favorite subject matter of innumerable pieces of literature, architecture, paintings, and sculptures. In every possible way, artists were trying to connect with and capture the strength and resolve of these unusual characters.

As with any story of human triumph, people saw the best of themselves in Jesus and Mary and yearned to find that perfection within themselves. Before Constantine and his horrid dream of conquering the world in the name of Christ, the true story of Jesus and Mary was out in the open for all to witness. In choosing to unite his kingdom under Christianity, Constantine delivered a fatal blow to the original Jesus movement. The incredible love story of Jesus and Mary was all but lost in the colossal ruins of the Roman Empire, only to be replaced by an entirely mythical narrative of the "Son of God" and his grieving mother.

HIDDEN IN PLAIN SIGHT

One might wonder why someone would go to such great lengths to conceal a man's simple, earthly, human existence - although, in the case of Jesus, the reason is obvious. With its entire foundation precariously resting on the presumption that Jesus was the "Son of God" sent to save mankind, the Church was compelled to go on a mission to seek and destroy all heretical scriptures that did not serve its purpose. Any evidence suggesting that Jesus was a man had to be eliminated.

Unlike other art forms, literature readily submits itself to all kinds of subtle manipulations. This was a fact that served the Church well in expanding its religious empire by glorifying and sanctifying people's beliefs. In a world where the majority didn't know how to read or write and were fearful of all forms of authority, especially the one ordained by God, fanciful imaginations were easily passed off as truth.

Armed with its new politically-motivated doctrine, Roman Christianity was self-assured in its ambitious plans of conquering the world in the name of God. It was certain that the illiterate, emotionally vulnerable masses had no other option but to submit to the book; if not, there was always the sword.

Trying to find Jesus inside Christianity is like trying to find a needle in a stack of needles. Within its self-reflecting prism walls, he is everywhere and nowhere at the same time. To have any chance of understanding the Jesus story, we have to begin by untangling ourselves from the sticky web of Christian theology. To meet the real Jesus and Mary, we have to move away from the scriptures and dive into the world of visual storytelling, where the memory of their incredible lives is preserved in vivid detail in some of the world's most beautiful works of art.

Stories captured in symbolisms of artworks such as paintings and sculptures are better sources of history than even scriptures, for unlike words, they cannot easily be manipulated to suit one's personal motives. After all, it isn't possible to delete and add a new paragraph to a statue. In fact, the only way to alter an original artwork without destroying it altogether is by altering the story surrounding it, and in the case of Jesus, that is exactly what happened.

Stepping into the picture almost four hundred years after Jesus, Roman Christianity supplied its own narrative to the existing images of the Jesus movement. If only we can avoid falling into mental grooves created by centuries of biblical storytelling, we can shed some light on the extraordinary human lives of Jesus and Mary with the help of the rich visual art that already exists.

A careful study of early Christian art reveals, beyond any doubt, that Jesus was neither a divine being nor a figment of people's imagination. He was a fully flesh and blood human teacher. Some of the earliest images of Jesus depict him as a young man flaunting a beard and long, flowing hair that is parted in the middle. He is often seen in the company of his twelve disciples, and almost always depicted carrying a book.

The unique symbols that help us identify Jesus, which are always a part of his imagery, point not to an imaginary figure, but to a real human being. The historical Jesus had to be an ordinary man with uniquely recognizable facial features - otherwise, there would have been no necessity for artists to stay true to his image, which has remained remarkably consistent over the centuries.

While an enlightened man's teachings alone should testify to his earthly roots, without the help of visual art to capture some of Jesus' characteristic physical features, it would have been easier to conclude that he was nothing more than a figment of the Jewish imagination.

Without over-exerting our mental faculties, we can see that it isn't impossible for a man like Jesus to have walked among us. There is no need to bring in unnecessary conflict between his earthly life and his seemingly otherworldly teachings. As a man, Jesus would have been perfectly capable of falling in love, marrying, and having children. At the same time, the Truth he had found within himself would have given him the authority to influence people's lives in a profound way.

Even fully devoted Christians will have to, at some point, embrace the fact that Jesus lived and died as an ordinary man, and not just pretending to be human. The stubborn refusal to accept this is the starting point of all conflicts between the images of the historical Jesus who was a man, and the biblical Jesus who is the "Son of God."

The biggest disagreement between believers and non-believers has always been the idea that three days after his crucifixion, Jesus came back to life and bodily ascended to heaven - a belief that is the beating heart of Christianity. If even a single strand of Jesus' hair were ever discovered, the whole idea of resurrection would crumble to dust, perhaps taking down with it the faith it supports.

One woman, absolutely hated by the Church, can unravel the truth of Jesus' life, both before and after his death. She alone has the power to affirm that Jesus was an ordinary man in every sense of the term. By stripping Mary Magdalene of her dignity and her rightful place in history, Roman Christianity had assumed that it had done enough to silence her voice.

One of the earliest images of Jesus

Despite over two millennia of religious plotting, scheming, and screaming, Mary Magdalene's silence can be heard louder than all the words of biblical theology put together. It is inevitable that someday Mary Magdalene's truth will explode on the canvas of human consciousness, challenging the beliefs of a mighty religious empire built on an erroneous interpretation of one woman's internalization of her teacher's words.

In the entirety of Christian history, no other individual has troubled the Church more than Mary Magdalene - to the extent that it had to stoop to the levels of carrying out an enormous cover-up of works, including scriptural alterations and deletions and the invention of purely imaginary characters in order to fit Mary inside its theology. The craftiness with which the Church has handled the Mary problem is a unique undertaking in all of human history.

During the first three hundred years of Christianity, no other personality of the Jesus movement was revered and worshiped as much as Mary Magdalene, whose churches had sprung up everywhere. As Jesus' beloved disciple, his wife, and the Mother of the Church, Mary occupied a central place in early Christian rituals and artworks. Owing to the two different time periods of her life, Mary's image had branched off into two uniquely recognizable artistic representations. In one, she was depicted as a young mother holding her newborn child in her arms; and in the other, as an older woman standing beside her daughter Sarah.

Arriving almost four hundred years later, Roman Christianity had to explain these worship traditions of Mary without denting the "Son of God" image of Jesus. Unable to accept Mary Magdalene's truth, it conjured up two entirely fictitious characters to aid in the cover-up process.

With utter disregard for history and facts, under the conveniently distorted logic of the Catholic doctrine, the younger Mary became Jesus' mother and the older Mary, his grandmother. Both the Virgin Mary and St. Anne are Catholic scriptural offshoots of the original mother of the Jesus movement, Mary Magdalene. For over a thousand years, under different names, Catholic Christians have been worshiping the same Mary - the Magdalene whom the Church called a repentant whore.

One might wonder, if both Jesus' mother and grandmother are fictional characters invented to fill the gaps in Catholic doctrine, then where do we get their Bible stories from? It is interesting to note that while there are some references to Jesus' mother in the Bible, there is absolutely nothing mentioned about her in any of the original gospels recorded by Jesus' disciples. It isn't just a coincidence that both Jesus' mother and his wife are named Mary. There was only one Mary in the Jesus story who mattered, and she wasn't his mother.

Not surprisingly, the Gnostic Gospels and the New Testament are also completely silent about St. Anne, the supposed grandmother of Jesus. The original source for these stories isn't history, but ancient Jewish myths. The image of the Virgin Mary comes from the Jewish book of Isaiah: "Behold, the virgin shall conceive and bear a son, and they shall call his name Immanuel." The word "virgin" simply meant, a "young woman." Similarly, St. Anne drew her image from a Jewish woman, Hannah, who, according to the story, was desperate for a child and was visited by God to bless her womb with a baby girl. Both of these Jewish stories come from a time long before Jesus.

As vehemently as we have argued that Jesus is the "Son of God" sent to redeem our lost souls, the fact remains that, like any of us, he was an ordinary man - a human teacher, husband, and father. None can testify to this fact more fully than Mary Magdalene -

Jesus' wife, favorite disciple, and the mother of his children. There is a reason why Mary Magdalene is the most despised woman of the Christian world, whom Pope Gregory once called "a sinful woman who perfumes her flesh in forbidden acts."

While the Church has done everything in its power to conceal the real identity of Jesus by erasing any evidence pointing to his human nature, Mary Magdalene has always held the keys to exposing it all. Even to this day, she guards one of the greatest secrets hidden from mankind - one that has been at the heart of humanity's most vicious of all religious conflicts - a secret so powerful that when revealed, it can shake the very foundations of Christianity.

The ultimate justice to the Jesus story is in attempting to free Mary from the theological cages of Christianity where she has been unjustly trapped for the past two thousand years - if only to see her fly away and take her rightful place beside Jesus, as his beloved wife and the only witness to his truth.

Despite the Church's best attempts to undermine her importance, having denigrated her to the lowest possible status of a repentant whore, the gut-wrenching story of Mary's bleeding heart has left an indelible mark on the human psyche. As little as we know about Mary through Christian scriptures, she is everywhere in the world of art. Perhaps there has never been another human being who has captured the imagination of free-spirited artists, quite like her.

Mary Magdalene occupies a unique place in the collective consciousness of our past. She dwells in that twilight zone of human emotions, between admiration and loathing, pity and contempt, fact and fiction - an undefined mental space that is the favorite playground of free creative spirits. Of all the artists Mary has been able to inspire, she has had the greatest influence on one colossal creative genius - the sage of high renaissance art, the master himself, Leonardo da Vinci.

RENAISSANCE MAN

Art is a silent cry of the human spirit, knocking at the doors of the mind and body in an attempt to break free. Human civilization and all that it has accomplished are byproducts of this inner stirring. There is something inside us, beyond the recognizable physical phenomenon of life, that compels us to be creators and lovers of art. There is a reason why we feel perfectly at home while either creating something or admiring its artistic beauty. Nothing moves the human spirit like melodiously composed music, an intriguing painting, or a beautiful piece of poetry. Human art should be definitive proof that the source of creation is not somewhere out there in heaven, but right here within us.

The rich and myriad forms of human art remind us that we are not an end product of creation, but its continuous living and breathing center. We are the extended limbs of existence, aiding it in its process of creation. This is why we cannot be content with what we have without knowing who we are.

Our quest for perfection is a calling of our inner creative self to recognize its presence. This is what gives meaning, purpose, and grandness to life. Without this inner center contributing its eternal spiritual qualities, life is nothing more than a play of light and shadows. Everything we recognize as beautiful, both inside and outside of ourselves, comes from here. While most of us live and die aimlessly circling around this creative center, there comes a man like da Vinci, who plunges into its inner sanctum to become the very definition of the word "art."

A piece of art, as enchanting as it may be, can never surpass, in its beauty and grandeur, the spirit of the artist who breathed life into it. The best of artistic expressions, be it a painting, a sculpture, a musical composition, or a piece of literature, bear not only the unique signature of the ephemeral mind and body of the artist, but also the silent cry of their immortal spirit.

Even after more than five hundred years of familiarity, da Vinci's works, especially his paintings, continue to intrigue us, not because they emerged from the brush strokes of a crafty artist or rose from the depths of his sweeping intellect, but mainly because they were works of a free-spirited individual who thirsted to share with the world something far more important than just his artistic gifts.

If creating art is about exploring the uncharted realms of life and the laws of nature that govern it - if it is about pushing the human intellect beyond the boundaries of the known and the unknown, to toil in loneliness and obscurity, striving to leave one's artistic footprints on the sands of time - if it is about standing by the side of love, truth, and wisdom to lend voice to the silenced and the forgotten, then da Vinci must be remembered not just as an artist but as someone who redefined the meaning of the word "art."

It is hard to measure the true genius of a man like da Vinci, for it wasn't limited to any one specific area of expertise. Although we know him mostly as a master painter, da Vinci was an equally well-accomplished anatomist, scientist, architect, engineer, and writer.

Never a prisoner of his accumulated wealth of knowledge or its looming shadow of self-importance, da Vinci flowed effortlessly between seemingly unrelated streams of knowledge. Like a meandering river unaffected by the past or the future, he lived and moved in the present, endlessly discovering newer, more intimate ways of navigating the maze of life.

Of all things, da Vinci's extraordinary success as an artist must be attributed to his highly informal and unconventional early education. His genius represents one of the finest examples of a human intellect that managed to escape the smothering blanket of social and religious conformity of its time.

The fact that he invented an entirely new style of writing just for keeping notes affirms the untethered, individualistic upbringing of da Vinci. Except for those rare occasions when he intended for his text to be read and understood by others, he almost exclusively wrote in a backward mirror script from right to left.

It is unclear why da Vinci developed this style of writing. Either he was trying to make it harder for people to steal his ideas or, being left-handed, it simply came naturally to him to write like this. But, most likely, he did this just to be different - a case of da Vinci being his usual rebellious self, questioning the rigidity of language and displaying his well-known disdain for imitation.

Everything we know about da Vinci suggests that he was averse to all forms of restrictions, whether physical, intellectual, social, or religious, that posed a threat to individual freedom. He loved freedom so much that he was renowned for his peculiar habit of buying caged birds and them free, just to watch them fly away.

Freedom was a foundational philosophy of da Vinci's life, but his idea of freedom wasn't limited to his personal experiences or memories alone. It was an all-encompassing concept that he derived from his love for nature and the natural order of the universe. He was an ardent admirer of nature and one of her most devoted students.

As much as da Vinci tried to capture the enchanting beauty of nature in his paintings, he also endeavored to emulate her enigmatic ways. We catch glimpses of the nature of this relationship even in such seemingly simple instructions where he writes, "A painter should begin every canvas with a wash of black, because all things in nature are dark except where exposed by the light."

Who can say with absolute certainty that these are solely da Vinci's words and not nature speaking through him? After all, an artist is nothing more than an extension of nature - a brushstroke of her imagination. Nature is not only an artist's favorite playground but also one of their best-kept secrets of inspiration. As da Vinci stated, she is "the mistress of all masters."

When we examine da Vinci's life's work in its entirety, it is challenging not to observe how spectacularly different his paintings are, in terms of both their intended purpose and impact, when compared to his other artistic endeavors. It's almost as if da Vinci the painter is altogether different from da Vinci the scientist, anatomist, writer, and architect. The most apparent and streaking peculiarity is, of course, the unusual subject matter of his paintings, with more than half of all his known works dedicated to one overarching theme: the portrayal of biblical scenes from the Christian storytelling tradition.

This unusual creative choice of da Vinci raises an all-important and often overlooked question: why would an eternally inquisitive seeker of knowledge, dedicated to pursuing objective, verifiable, scientific truths of nature, spend a better part of his adult life striving to bring ancient religious stories to life?

The answer to this question may seem obvious if we view da Vinci as merely another Renaissance painter influenced by the most prevalent artistic themes of his era. However, everything we understand about da Vinci suggests that he was unlikely to pursue an area of interest unless something personally drove him to explore its hidden mysteries.

In addition to familiarity, there must have been another, more compelling reason motivating da Vinci to dedicate as much time as he did, pouring his life into what is now universally recognized as "Christian art." Devotion to Jesus or his miracles is undoubtedly not among those reasons we can imagine. The deeply rational mind of da Vinci, rooted in truth and experience, would have categorically dismissed such a romanticized interpretation of a man's life.

It isn't hard to guess whom and what da Vinci is referring to when he says, "Many have made a trade of delusions and false miracles, deceiving the stupid multitudes." Besides, how can a truth-seeking, freedom-loving, critical thinker like da Vinci accept the authority of an institution like the Church that was mercilessly trampling on the one thing he valued most - human freedom?

During one of his prophetic moods, da Vinci writes, "There will appear gigantic figures in human shape, but the nearer you get to them, the more their immense stature will diminish." Perhaps more than anything else, this is what he was attempting to do with his paintings - get as close as possible to the real lives of these ancient biblical characters, to bring them down from the high altar of religious misrepresentation to their simple, original, relatable human form.

While the Church had managed to convince the gullible masses that the Holy Bible and its innumerable artistic interpretations were depicting the life of a divine being, da Vinci was aware, beyond any doubt, that in the images of Jesus and Mary, we were looking at a wholly flesh and blood human story.

This fundamental conflict between da Vinci and the Church - between the approaches of science and religion - between truth and myth, is what gives us some of the most mysterious, philosophically loaded paintings in the world. Commissioned to paint popular biblical themes by rich and powerful patrons of Christian art, da Vinci brings these exquisite works to light in his own characteristic style, combining some of the best-known painting techniques to give us a rare glimpse into the conveniently forgotten human lives of Jesus and Mary.

With the obvious intention of hiding his secrets from the Church, he subtly and craftily embeds his messages within the more familiar narrative of his paintings, taking full advantage of the fact that

Christians have always assumed they know what they are looking at in any biblical artwork.

This is what makes da Vinci's paintings so mysterious. He is secretly trying to tell us something, and we never tire of trying to figure out what that is. Some may argue that we might simply be imagining all this, adding more than what he intended us to see, although this is to miss the whole point of why he created these works in the first place.

Not all who are drawn to Christian art necessarily come for the divine stories of Jesus and Mary. Some have been curious about the human lives shaping their myth. The naturally inquisitive mind of da Vinci would have reveled in the idea of exploring and exposing some of these secrets. Besides, what better way to mock the authority of the Church than by elegantly smearing your truth all over it.

The Greatest Love Story Never Told

NAKED AND UNPRETENTIOUS

The Penitent Magdalene

In the church of Santa Croce, Florence, where da Vinci was christened, stood a fine polychrome wooden statue of Mary Magdalene. It was a sculpture visibly influenced by Donatello's "Penitent Magdalene" - an exquisitely carved, unusually realistic, one-of-a-kind masterpiece - most likely da Vinci's first introduction to the realism of high renaissance art. Imagined distinctly apart from her usual mythical representation, Donatello's Mary Magdalene is as real as she gets.

Her body ravaged by time and nature, Mary stands in her usual penitent pose, peering through those deep sunken eyes that display every possible human frailty of a life eagerly awaiting death. Clothed in nothing but her own flowing hair, she appears to be naturally growing from the wood on which she is carved. There is something extraordinarily raw and primal about this image of Mary. Like an old dying tree, she is naked and unpretentious, blissfully clinging to both life and death at the same time.

This is one of those rare, hard-hitting, impossible-to-forget art pieces that immediately stops one's chain of thought to make room for the question, "Who is this woman, and why does she look like that?"

The fact that Mary Magdalene spent the last thirty years of her life alone in a cave, far away from all things human, would have intrigued the mind of a mystical, nature-loving da Vinci, compelling him to dive in and explore everything he can about this lonely, discarded woman who appears to have sprung from the very bosom of the earth. It would not have taken long for an artist like da Vinci to get to the bottom of the truth that both Mary Magdalene and Mary, the supposed mother of Jesus are one and the same individual.

Da Vinci's fascination with this young widow, whom early Christians fondly referred to as "Mother Mary," went much further than just an artistic fixation. His love affair with her was rooted in a far deeper personal connection. Da Vinci's mother, Caterina, was a poor, lower-class woman whom Ser Piero da Vinci could not marry because of her status. Da Vinci grew up as the illegitimate son of this peasant woman, who was pregnant with him when she was only fifteen.

Just like Mary Magdalene, Caterina was a fallen woman. In the tender, loving image of young Mary, da Vinci saw his own mother. She would eventually become his biggest obsession, inspiring some of the most mysterious works of art ever created by the hand of man.

There is no way to know what Jesus or Mary looked like. Scriptures offer nothing to aid us in the imagination of their physical features. And yet, going by their representation in art alone, we can conclude that early Christians saw Jesus more like a teacher, and

Mary as a grieving wife and a mother caring for her newborn child.

This ability to capture and preserve trinkets of individuality, to offer us a window into the forgotten lives of the past, is the single biggest contribution of art to humanity. An art form, such as a painting or a sculpture, can symbolically preserve unique finger-prints of individuality much better than written scriptures.

While stories captured in words can be endlessly altered with little regard for historical accuracy, it is far more difficult to manipulate art because it draws its inspiration not from our self-centered mind, but someplace deeper. That's why it is easier to introduce a fictitious Joseph into the scriptures to fill the gaps in the biblical narrative than to secure him a spot next to Mary in the world of visual art.

While artists have relied heavily on symbolisms to accurately capture the life and times of the subjects they are dealing with, da Vinci has used symbols for an altogether different purpose - to cleverly conceal, and sometimes reveal, the true identity of his characters. Perhaps, no other master has wielded the power of this artistic tool more elegantly and craftily than da Vinci.

A deeper exploration of da Vinci's paintings reveals a fascinating underplay of subtle artistic symbolisms, subliminally narrating an altogether different tale from the one intended to be more obvious. It is here, in the mystical space between perception and reality where da Vinci's true genius dwells, we can discover the real identity of a woman to whom he dedicated some of his life's finest works.

While the Bible has been silent about the real Mary Magdalene, her life has been captured in some of the most uniquely identifiable artistic symbolisms. In sculptures and paintings, Mary can be unmistakably recognized by her flowing curls, the Jewish mourning attire she wore, the natural rocky mountainous backdrop against which she is usually set, and in the company of a book and an alabaster jar - symbolisms, all of which would resurface in da Vinci's mysterious paintings.

A FAMILY PORTRAIT

The Virgin and Child with St. Anne

Da Vinci's genius has been evident right from the beginning, but the work that definitively introduces us to da Vinci the master storyteller and philosopher is an intriguing, full-size charcoal drawing known as "The Burlington House Cartoon" - also sometimes referred to as "The Virgin and Child with St. Anne and St. John the Baptist." This unfinished drawing, most probably an early sketch of a painting commissioned to be the high altarpiece of a church in Florence, is supposed to be depicting a well-known scene of baby Jesus playing on the laps of his mother and grandmother, as his cousin, St. John the Baptist, looks on.

At first glance, this may look like a typical Christian artwork attempting to capture a moment in the life of infant Jesus. However, a deeper exploration reveals some obvious and glaring inconsistencies. The first thing that strikes us is how simple, human, and non-dramatic the drawing is, especially considering that it deals entirely with religious subject matter.

There also seems to be a perceptible disconnect between the overall mood of the drawing and the story it is trying to tell us. In one of the most daring uses of artistic symbolisms, da Vinci places Mary directly on the lap of St. Anne, setting an all-new precedent in religious art for capturing an intimate relationship between two grown women, especially a mother and her daughter.

Da Vinci makes no attempt to clearly establish what should have been an obvious age difference between the two women. St. Anne doesn't look any older than Mary and she is also, for no apparent reason, recognizably taller. Perhaps the most fascinating feature of the drawing is the expression he manages to capture on the face of St. Anne, re-affirming its mysterious nature and introducing us to the incomprehensible genius of da Vinci.

What appears to be a look of a mother's admiration toward her daughter is, in fact, that unmistakable masculine gaze that gently floats between love and lust before deciding on which one to alight. The better we understand this unusual sketch, the easier it is to conclude that there is an obvious conflict between what we are seeing and what da Vinci intends to show. If only we can go beyond our biblical conditioning and see this drawing for what it truly represents, all the inconsistencies disappear at once, giving rise to an entirely different artwork.

While we have always assumed this to be a religious sketch of the Virgin Mary and St. Anne, da Vinci is presenting us with something else altogether. This masterpiece in storytelling, which reveals more about the relationship between Jesus and Mary than the entire Bible put together, is quite simply a sketch of Mary Magdalene sitting on the lap of Jesus and playing with her two children.

SHE WAS THERE

The Last Supper

If there was ever a piece of art meant to be read like a book, imparting new meaning every time we came back to it, to revel in exploring its unending mysteries, it has to be "The Last Supper" - the artistic colossus of da Vinci - one of the world's most celebrated paintings.

This powerful masterpiece, depicting Jesus' last meal with his disciples, fittingly adorns the end wall of the dining hall at the monastery of Santa Maria delle Grazie in Milan, Italy - occupying a sacred space where da Vinci the artist and da Vinci the philosopher secretly met to conspire and create what is undoubtedly one of the world's most mysterious works of art.

Despite its severely deteriorated condition, it's hard not to notice how realistic, visceral, and emotionally charged this painting is. As if struck by an invisible whirlwind of emotion that has uprooted their spirits, all the characters in the painting are swinging and swaying, struggling to deal with the weight of the moment. With each and every part of their being - their hands, eyes, feet, and torsos screaming in dissent - one can almost smell the chaotic tension in the room.

While it has always been assumed that these are the reactions of the disciples to Jesus announcing that he would be betrayed by one of them, the intensity of their reactions and their facial expressions suggests something else altogether. After all, da Vinci would not have taken all this trouble to show us something we already know. For its overly melodramatic, prophetic tone alone, da Vinci would have rejected the interpretation that Jesus somehow knew he would be betrayed. The whole story of Judas betraying Jesus for a few silver coins was fabricated and inserted into the gospels to shift the blame for Jesus' death away from the Romans and onto the Jews.

Far from being a betrayer, Judas was one of Jesus' closest disciples, who actually understood his master's teachings. He was also related to Jesus, and managed the finances of the entire group - a fact da Vinci acknowledges by placing a money sack in his hand.

In fact, if there was anyone who betrayed Jesus by totally misunderstanding and misinterpreting his teachings, it was the hardheaded Simon Peter, on whose barren rock rests the foundation of the Christian faith. If there is any doubt as to where da Vinci stood in his opinion of the Church and its mission, he clears it all out in one sweeping image of Peter, presenting him as a two-faced scheming and plotting serpent cleverly concealing his true motive - a knife in his grotesquely twisted hand.

The first three synoptic Gospels - Mathew, Mark, and Luke - all present a very similar, familiar religious interpretation of Jesus' last supper. It is only the fourth gospel, by one "Beloved Disciple" John, that departs from the usual prophetic tone of the Bible to give us a very different spiritual account of the meeting.

For obvious reasons, the real gender and identity of this disciple were deliberately concealed. The figure sitting to the right of Jesus, distinctly recognizable by her feminine face and flowing hair, and usually misidentified as John, is none other than Jesus' wife and spiritual companion, Mary Magdalene. Da Vinci's "Last Supper" is a painting whose subject matter directly concerns this forgotten woman - the "Beloved Disciple" of Jesus.

One can hardly think of another biblical artwork celebrating Mary's life, her crucial role in the Jesus movement, and the complex relationship she shared with Jesus and the other disciples, quite like "The Last Supper." This artistic whirlwind of da Vinci distinguishes itself from every other "Last Supper" painting out there, if only in its ability to capture intricate human relationships.

Da Vinci lets these biblical figures tell their own stories, guided simply by how and where they are positioned in the painting. For instance, he sets Jesus, Mary, and Judas right at the center, their bodies branching out like petals of the same flower around an imaginary center shaped by the coming together of their hands, symbolically stating that all three were related to each other. Judas was the son of Martha, Mary Magdalene's sister.

Furthermore, using the image of Judas - his right arm resting on the table and his exposed neck and shoulder region - da Vinci does something unthinkable. He gives us an image that irrefutably proves that Jesus and Mary were indeed husband and wife.

Right in the middle of an intense emotional drama being played out between a somewhat disappointed teacher and his angry students, da Vinci quietly introduces us to the newest member of the Jesus family in almost a whisper, so as not to disturb the mood of the moment. On a colossal painting measuring almost thirty feet in width, hiding in plain sight like a scar drawn on the face of the Church, da Vinci sets on the table the earthly seed of Jesus and Mary's love in flesh and blood.

As hard as it may be to stumble upon it accidentally when one isn't looking for it, once spotted, it's almost impossible to forget that there is a baby on the serving table of "The Last Supper." Morphed as Judas' arm and neck, the infant, wrapped in blue, is looking straight at Andrew who has both his hands up as if to say, "Please don't come to me."

Perhaps here, da Vinci is having some fun alluding to the fact that Andrew was one of those rare disciples of Jesus who had chosen to remain single; but, more importantly, he is suggesting that Jesus was married, and he was a father.

While it may seem like da Vinci is taking all this trouble just to bring out the suppressed and forgotten human side of Jesus, more crucially, he is establishing the fact that Mary Magdalene, far from being some low-life sinner, was an integral and influential member of the Jesus community.

As an intelligent and resourceful woman, favorite disciple, and wife of Jesus, Mary held a position lesser in importance only to Jesus himself. As is the case with almost every other biblical painting of da Vinci, the central theme of "The Last Supper" revolves not so much around Jesus as it does around Mary.

The single biggest clue da Vinci leaves to subtly tell us what this painting is all about, hides in the conflict he manages to capture between Peter and Mary - two diametrically opposed personalities of the Jesus Movement who differed from each other in almost every way, especially in their understanding of Jesus and his message.

While Mary understood the symbolic meaning in Jesus' words to recognize him as a teacher, Peter could only see him as a religious messiah sent to fulfill the Jewish prophecy of bringing God's kingdom to earth - a literal, physical interpretation that put him in direct conflict with Mary's spiritual understanding of Jesus.

Considering her important status and obvious closeness to Jesus, Peter mostly tolerated Mary, occasionally even approving of her, but secretly he despised everything about this strong, independent, spiritually gifted woman. Da Vinci captures this conflict beautifully by showing Peter affectionately leaning over Mary while secretly hiding a knife.

The most obvious challenge in accurately interpreting any artwork, especially a famous painting, is imagining more than what the artist is intending to say. While this is true in almost every case, with da Vinci however, the problem is quite the opposite. Even when stretched to their absolute creative limits, our imaginations fall short of fully comprehending the storytelling genius of da Vinci.

We have a hard time accepting the fact that it is indeed possible for a master painter to wield his paintbrush like a pen, to share more than what we can possibly understand. Just like a writer thirsting to tell his story, da Vinci uses every inch of his painting to speak his mind. There are no "empty spaces" in a da Vinci painting - even when he appears to be silent, he is telling us something. One of the finest examples of this art of silent subliminal storytelling is da Vinci's depiction of Mary in "The Last Supper."

In an emotionally intense painting that relies mainly on the reactions of the disciples to tell the story, da Vinci introduces us to a Mary who is utterly devoid of emotions. Far from reacting to the unfolding chaos, she is entirely silent. Like the eye of a raging storm, Mary quietly sits in the middle, in a serene, meditative mood, half awake and half asleep to everything happening around her.

On its own, this image of Mary is quite unremarkable, but when seen from the context of the overly masculine mood of the painting, it stands out as one of the most powerful representations of the feminine - so much so that it forces us to conclude that as far as da Vinci is concerned, the central figure of this painting isn't Jesus, but Mary. Ironically, da Vinci is using his artistic skills to conceal the real identity of Mary in a painting that adorns the walls of the very church dedicated to worshiping her.

There is a reason why Mary is unaffected by Jesus' words. It is the very same reason why Peter, despite his resentment, is attempting to keep Mary's company, why Philip is looking at her with an expression of deep reverence and acceptance, and why da Vinci is bending backward to share her forgotten story.

For centuries, we have regarded the Last Supper as that all-important event during which Jesus predicted his betrayal and crucifixion, thereby decisively proving his divinity. However, none of the earliest gospels chronicling the event mention anything about this premonition. Far from capturing an over-simplified religious dialogue, the original Gnostic Gospels written by some of Jesus' closest disciples provide a detailed spiritual account of this meeting.

Jesus didn't have to be a clairvoyant prophet to foresee his impending doom. He knew that he was a troublemaker and had gone a little too far with his temper tantrums at the Jewish temple. Knowing well that he could be captured any time, he spends his last few precious moments addressing some of the concerns of his disciples - the most important one being the future of the community and its leadership in his absence.

The Gnostic Gospels document Jesus giving a longer-than-usual spiritual discourse, washing the feet of the disciples to express his love, and making an extraordinary announcement - one that would set in motion a series of events that would forever alter the course of human history.

Jesus comforts his distraught disciples and assures them that he is not abandoning them, as he has chosen a "helper" who will guide and lead them after he is gone. The Last Supper is an event remembered by early Christians as that definitive moment when Jesus, to the utter dismay of his disciples, points to Mary and says, "Behold thy mother," introducing her as their teacher for the first time.

Da Vinci's "The Last Supper" depicts the moment of dissent between Jesus and his disciples, capturing, in vivid detail, that long-forgotten image of Jesus' betrayal: grown men sitting around a fully awakened man, their minds drenched in his spiritual words of wisdom but their hearts dry and empty, trembling in fear at the very thought of accepting a woman as their teacher.

THE SECRET OF HER SMILE

Mona Lisa

The world's most famous painting is a half portrait of a woman whose enigmatic smile has haunted the human race for over five centuries. Despite its unusually small size and eerie simplicity, "Mona Lisa" is quintessential da Vinci - a stunningly detailed, anatomically near-perfect specimen of the human form captured in all its resplendent natural grace and elegance.

And yet, what makes the Mona Lisa special isn't her exquisitely crafted smile, but the secret she guards behind it. We are drawn to her because she is one of the most mysterious, least understood obsessions of da Vinci - because we are yet to convincingly answer that all-important question, "Who is da Vinci's Mona Lisa?"

According to a sixteenth-century biography of da Vinci by Giorgio Vasari, she is Madam Lisa Gherardini, the wife of a wealthy merchant who commissioned the painting to celebrate the construction of his new house and the birth of his second son. However, there is no reason to unquestionably accept this historical account as a confirmation of Mona Lisa's true identity, particularly given the fact that da Vinci almost never worked on and completed the exact same painting he was originally commissioned to produce, without somehow making it his own.

If this were to be any other painting by any other artist, a simple, straightforward origin narrative might have sufficed; but with da Vinci, it is only the beginning of a long story - one that would stretch far beyond the end of his life.

"Mona Lisa" was no ordinary painting. She was da Vinci's single biggest obsession, consuming more time and energy than anything else he had labored to create. To put things in perspective, while it took da Vinci three years to complete his biggest wall mural, "The Last Supper," it would take him no less than four years to complete the first draft of "Mona Lisa" - a relatively small painting one hundred times smaller.

It is utterly nonsensical to think that da Vinci's most loved painting, the one he spent the last fifteen years of his life striving to perfect, and that was still in his possession when he died, is a portrait of some unknown Italian noblewoman whose only admirable quality happened to be the fact that she was the wife of a wealthy Florentine silk merchant.

If a da Vinci painting is silent, it can only mean one of two things: either we do not understand it, or it isn't a da Vinci painting. To say that "Mona Lisa" is nothing more than an elegantly crafted piece of art - not a philosophically or personally motivated expression of individuality, but a faithful reproduction of a commissioned work - is an outright insult to the creative genius of da Vinci and everything he stood for.

"Mona Lisa" is silent, not because she has nothing to say, but only because she was never meant to be understood by all. It is easy to forget that this thirty-inch portrait, now the world's most visited artwork, wasn't created to be hung in the middle of a crowded hallway for all to admire, understand, and fall in love with.

"Mona Lisa" wasn't just another painting created for the world. She was the consummation of an extraordinary journey of one man's obsession with truth - a deeply personal love letter da Vinci wrote to himself, immortalizing a woman who inspired some of his life's finest works.

Perhaps the only other question more puzzling than Mona Lisa's mysterious identity is the reason why da Vinci went to such great lengths to conceal it. It could be a case of da Vinci wanting to create an impossible-to-read, truly personal artwork that only he can fully understand and appreciate, or it might just be that "Mona Lisa" is only a part of a much bigger secret.

To have any chance at understanding what da Vinci is trying to tell us here, we have to first accept the fact that the "Mona Lisa" was no ordinary painting. She was a deeply intimate work of a master painter who had at his disposal every available skill accumulated over a lifetime spent understanding the human phenomenon.

We can finally solve this five-hundred-year-old da Vinci riddle, provided we are willing to forget everything we know about "Mona Lisa" and look at her again for the first time, not as the world's most famous painting, but as da Vinci's most personal.

It is hard to look at the "Mona Lisa" and not wonder, "How is it even possible for this half-portrait of a woman, unremarkable in almost every way, to be the world's most celebrated artwork?" To begin with, Mona Lisa isn't even particularly beautiful. In fact, with her unusually prominent brow ridges, ghostly pale skin, and almost nonexistent eyebrows, she looks more mythical than real.

Besides, for some strange reason, she is missing all the fashion extravagances that define a typical fifteenth-century Florentine lady of means. Thanks to her master's unparalleled artistic wizardry, Mona Lisa can still pass for a wealthy merchant's wife, but a deeper understanding of the painting reveals that da Vinci is pointing us in an entirely different direction.

"Mona Lisa" is more mysterious than we can possibly imagine. Taking extraordinary care not to make it too obvious and painstakingly pouring over her every delicate detail, da Vinci has embellished Mona Lisa with subtle artistic symbolisms that simultaneously reveal and hide her identity.

To begin with, Mona Lisa isn't wearing a typical gaudy French robe. Instead, she is dressed in a modest, somberly dark silk garment resembling one of those linen gowns worn by pregnant women. Most notably, a thin, almost transparent black veil covering her head and flowing curls runs across the entire length of her body in a style that is commonly seen in paintings of the Virgin Mary.

Further, da Vinci places Mona Lisa in front of a natural rocky mountainous backdrop and seats her in a serene and contented posture with her folded hands resting on the arm of the chair, which also subtly morphs into a lateral view of a book.

And finally, on the ledge behind her, camouflaged as the base of a wooden column, sits Mona Lisa's single biggest secret: an ancient-looking alabaster jar. Da Vinci's Mona Lisa is none other than the world's most famous woman - the Mother of the Christian Church, the Madonna of the lilies, Jesus' wife, Mary Magdalene.

"Mona Lisa" is only one half of a much bigger puzzle. The secret to her unusually restrained features, mysterious smile, and distinctly androgynous face hides in an entirely different painting - a forgotten masterpiece that shatters every known conception of artistic representation - da Vinci's ultimate philosophical statement.

OUT OF THE SHADOWS

Salvator Mundi

Holding the record as the world's most expensive painting ever sold at a public auction, identical in its proportions to the "Mona Lisa," and sometimes referred to as the male "Mona Lisa," "Salvator Mundi" is an enchanting half-portrait of Jesus showing him as the "Savior of the World" holding a crystal orb in one hand and offering a benediction with the other.

This heavily over-painted artwork, rediscovered, restored, and authenticated as an original da Vinci after almost five hundred years since its creation, is one of the most unusual paintings of Jesus. It did not emerge from the conforming heart of a believing Christian, but from the rebellious mind of a critical-thinking philosopher.

Da Vinci's paintings are an extension of his brilliantly lucid mind. They offer us a window into his carefully interwoven mental fabric of ideas, beliefs, and skills, standing for truth and its endearing sense of mystery, while striving to dispel some of our deep-rooted prejudices. "Salvator Mundi" appears to stand all alone as a painting that defies everything da Vinci believed in.

The most puzzling thing to understand is da Vinci's motivation for creating such a simple, straightforward, religious portrait of Jesus, working on it for almost eleven years at the peak of his artistic and philosophical prowess. Either we have completely misunderstood da Vinci and his beliefs, or "Salvator Mundi" is anything but a simple one-dimensional religious portrait of Jesus.

Any artist worth his salt who sincerely strives to emulate the mind of creation knows that form is an illusion. It is a play of light and shadows - an ever-changing perceptual duality oscillating between memory and imagination, dreams and nightmares, reality and illusion. If understanding this has been one of man's highest intellectual achievements, then capturing it in a painting, in all its splendid glory, has to be one of his greatest artistic accomplishments.

"Salvator Mundi," far from being just another religious portrait of Jesus, is a philosophical exposition on duality elegantly personified in human form. It is a one-of-a-kind masterpiece in visual dichotomy that settles, once and for all, the debate of Jesus' divinity by bringing together two lives separated by ignorance and injustice in one sweeping image. It is da Vinci's final, and arguably most daring act of rebellion against the Church.

While there's hardly a biblical painting by da Vinci that does not in some way illuminate the earthly life of Jesus, in "Salvator Mundi," he takes this to an all-new level, presenting Jesus as one half of an inseparable whole - the other occupied by his wife and beloved disciple, Mary Magdalene.

Using his signature artistic technique of anamorphosis - his ability to play with light and shadows to create images that defy human perception - da Vinci seamlessly integrates his understanding of the male and female form to give us a mysterious, unusually feminine portrait of Jesus. Of all the known artworks by da Vinci, only "Salvator Mundi" and "Mona Lisa" share a distinctly recognizable androgynous face.

The delicate face of Jesus, his oddly shaped chin and lips, smudged eyes, flowing golden hair, and his feminine gown, all perfectly align and blend as one in the image of Mona Lisa, as a simple superimposition of these two paintings confirms their physical proportions are mathematically identical. The reason "Salvator Mundi" appears feminine is the same reason "Mona Lisa" appears masculine; they both share the same face. "Salvator Mundi" and "Mona Lisa" are not two different paintings, but two different pieces of a single da Vinci puzzle.

The sheer magnitude of da Vinci's genius becomes apparent when we observe "Salvator Mundi" not from the front, like any other painting, but looking across from its extreme left side. When viewed from this odd angle, all the subtle, barely discernible feminine elements of the painting magically come together to reveal the familiar silhouette of a woman unmistakably recognizable by her androgynous face and mysterious smile. Like a primordial dream rising from the abysmal depths of time, Mary Magdalene, da Vinci's Mona Lisa, reluctantly steps out of the shadows to take her rightful place beside Jesus.

The Greatest Love Story Never Told

STILL TOGETHER

Shaped predominantly by her representation in art, the image of Mary occupies a unique place in our collective imagination, divided between two diametrically opposed, irreconcilable personalities of the venerable Mary and the repentant Magdalene.

While Mary is a beloved saint, revered as the mother of God and worshiped as a symbol of purity and chastity, Magdalene is often depicted as a fallen woman, living a life of penance and contemplation as a hermit. She exists in a world of her own, accompanied by only a few possessions - a book of Jesus' teachings, an alabaster jar, and a skull - remnants of her shattered dreams.

While the Church has done all it can to keep the chasm dividing these two images of Mary as deep and as wide as possible, convincing the masses that Mary and Magdalene are two entirely different individuals, one gruesome piece of evidence brings them together to remind us of the conveniently forgotten human tale of the severed lives of Jesus and Mary.

After almost two thousand years since she was unjustly separated from Jesus, banished from the holy land, and subjected to relentless persecution by a religio-political organization hell-bent on preserving its source of wealth and power, Mary Magdalene, to this day - even in her death, guards one of the biggest secrets hidden from mankind.

Her incredible story, preserved in unique artistic symbols adorning her countless paintings and sculptures, holds the key to exposing one of the biggest cover-ups in human history - a revelation that can utterly dismiss the claim that three days after he was shredded and hung on a cross to die, Jesus came back to life and bodily ascended to heaven.

Every now and then, a human story comes along that torments our imagination, finding its expression in artistic symbols that survive the trials and tribulations of time to become an inseparable part of our collective culture. While these symbols continue to evolve over time, adapting to shifting mindsets and changing narratives, can always be traced back to their original source, rooted in human memory.

Of all the symbols associated with bringing Mary Magdalene's tragic tale to light, one, in particular, stands out the most: the mysterious symbolism of a skull that is an inseparable part of Mary's imagery, captured in almost all her paintings. This same skull now sits in the hands of the "Virgin Mary" disguised as a globe, embellishing her Catholic image as the "Mother of God".

Mary Magdalene with the Skull

While it's easy to dismiss such odd symbolism as artistic imagination, perhaps used to personify Mary's grief, those who know anything at all about religious art will testify to the fact that the source of this unusual symbol, passed down through time, isn't imagination but memory.

There is something mysterious about the manner in which artists over the centuries have interpreted the image of this skull, with an extraordinary realism that is hard to miss. Unlike an imaginary symbol usually added as an afterthought, this skull of Mary, whenever present, almost always occupies a central place in her paintings, driving the entire narrative of her story. Most eerily, just like a real human skull detached from the rest of its body long ago, it is always depicted with a missing jawbone.

By far, one of the most compelling pieces of evidence supporting the fact that this is indeed a real human skull comes from Mary herself. Her unusual reverence and intimacy toward it have been stunningly captured in paintings and sculptures spanning centuries, which depict her talking to the skull, embracing it, staring into its empty sockets, praying, and wailing in front of it. This skull isn't just symbolizing Mary's suffering; it is the very object of her grief.

Truth is perhaps the only thing that continues to murmur long after it is silenced. At the dawn of the second millennium, almost exactly a thousand years after Jesus' crucifixion, a strange myth - more rooted in reality than one can possibly imagine - began to sweep across Europe.

The quest was for a lost biblical treasure - a religious artifact of immeasurable value known as the "Holy Grail." In all of history, there isn't another object, physical or ethereal, that has captured the human imagination, quite like the "Holy Grail" - so much so that the phrase has now transcended its limited meaning to become the very definition of all things "monumentally significant."

Even to this day, it is generally believed that the "Holy Grail" is some kind of a cup - apparently, the one Jesus drank from during his last supper. If this is indeed the case - if the world's most treasured artifact is nothing more than a cup - then the question that begs an explanation is: Why should this cup be more special than any other utensil Jesus ate or drank from, especially considering that any artifact even remotely associated with Jesus has to be immeasurably valuable?

Beyond the countless speculations and theories that have emerged around the legend of the "Holy Grail," one thing is certain: The Church was indeed searching for a lost artifact of Jesus, and had assigned the task of finding and safeguarding its secrets to one of its most powerful and influential military orders.

A deeper exploration of the stories surrounding the Grail reveals that there has always been a mysterious connection between the "Holy Grail," the Knights Templars, and Mary Magdalene. It isn't just a coincidence that the quest for the "Holy Grail" and the search for the lost relics of Mary Magdalene originated in the same region and during the same time period. The Church wasn't searching for some magical cup to add to its Vatican collection. It was searching for the sarcophagus of Mary Magdalene, believed to be the resting place of the Grail.

In December 1279, while pursuing the legend of her burial place, Charles II, King of Naples, unearthed the sarcophagus containing the body of Mary Magdalene. Found among her remains was the "Sainte Ampoule" - a glass vial containing earth soaked in blood collected by Mary at the foot of the cross.

Of all the unanswered questions surrounding the Grail, such as what triggered its quest in the first place or why the Church was dead-set on finding it before anyone else, the only two worth answering that can put to rest every speculation are: What is the "Holy Grail," and where is it now?

Unless it's true that Jesus bodily ascended to heaven, his mortal remains, or what's left of them, must still be here on earth hiding somewhere and waiting to be discovered. While the Bible gives us a wholly fictitious account of one Joseph of Arimathea, a member of the Sanhedrin, receiving the body of Jesus and dignifiedly entombing it in a garden cave, religious art passed down through memory captures the morbid mood of crucifixion, especially one woman's heart-rending cries of anguish, narrating an entirely different tale.

One of the most indelible images of the Jesus story, going all the way back to the hills of Calvary, is that of a young woman lamenting at the base of the cross, holding in her arms the shriveled body of her dead husband - an image seared into Christian memory and later immortalized by Michelangelo in his "Pieta."

Although the Bible grudgingly acknowledges that Mary Magdalene was present both during and after Jesus' crucifixion and that she was the first witness to his "Resurrection," it altogether ignores the fact that Mary was Jesus' wife - the one who received his lifeless body from the cross - and whose guttural screams were the prayer hymns of the early Christian church.

Michelangelo's Pieta

It is ironic that the Bible claims that the salvation of humanity rests on Jesus' suffering when, in fact, Christianity emerged almost entirely from the grief of one woman. The binding emotional thread of the early Christian faith wasn't the broken body of Jesus but the bleeding heart of Mary, the ghastly evidence of which is her thirty-year penance on a severed relic of Jesus she never let go of.

The Bible does get one thing right: Jesus' body did indeed disappear from Jerusalem - from the cave where it was laid to rest. But, contrary to belief, it did not ascend to heaven - it simply sailed on a vessel to another part of the world. The boat ferrying the three Marys that landed on the shores of Southern France was also carrying another precious cargo - the mortal remains of Jesus.

The story of Jesus' body arriving in France is preserved in an unbroken ancient tradition, according to which the relics were brought for safekeeping to the Roman Province of Gaul - modern-day Apt, near Marseille, where Mary Magdalene and the group first began teaching. The precious relics were buried in an underground crypt, a fact confirmed by the martyrology of Apt, one of the oldest in existence preserving such information.

Furthermore, fearing religious and political persecution, the first bishop of Apta Julia, St. Auspicius, moved these relics into a deeper subterranean chapel, not before carefully concealing all entrances leading to it. With time, with the church constructed over it falling into decay, and the location of this sacred treasure was all but lost.

At the close of the eighth century, after his decisive victory over the Saracens, Charlemagne returned to Apta Julia, taking upon himself the first task of re-consecrating its cathedral. The ceremony took place during Easter solemnities in a rather somber mood, for they had exhausted every effort to locate the exact spot of the underground crypt where St. Auspicius had buried the treasure they had been searching for.

The underground crypt

An enchanting, although exaggerated story preserved in the Catholic tradition as detailed by the Emperor in his letter to the Pope, recounts the events leading to the discovery of Jesus' relics - a story narrated in such palpable reverence and mystical grandeur that is only befitting a find of its magnitude.

According to the letter, "A young boy of fourteen, deaf, blind, and dumb, overcome by emotions, began to strike at the stairs of the altar of the church, urging them to dig at the spot. Unable to restrain the boy, and upon Charlemagne's instructions, the altar stairs were removed, revealing an entrance to a crypt sealed using large stones - the same chamber where St. Auspicius was known to perform the holy mass and feed his flock the bread of life.

The stones were removed and the boy began to run down the winding steps that lead to an underground church, now with the certainty of someone who can see and hear. He stopped at a walled recess, striking it to indicate that the treasure they sought was behind it. The wall was broken down to reveal another lower crypt at the end of a long narrow corridor lit by a burning lamp that flooded the place with unearthly splendor. The walled recess was thrown open and a sweet fragrance of Oriental balm filled the air. A casket of cypress wood was discovered containing the body, wrapped round and round in folds of precious cloth."

The Pope was immediately notified of the discovery, and major provinces of Gaul couldn't wait to solicit portions of the body thus discovered. Through the favors of powerful sovereigns, fragments of these precious remains found their way to various churches around France where they now rest in gold reliquaries, guarded by the Papal seal.

More than anybody else, it was the Catholic Church that was hell-bent on finding the buried remains of Jesus, not to share it with the world, but to hide them at any cost; for the very existence of this relic flew in the face of everything it had been preaching.

The forearm at the Shrine of St. Anne

While it would have been impossible to hide a discovery of this magnitude entirely, it was well within the prowess of the Church to conceal its true identity. For well over a millennium now, Catholics have been worshiping these relics as those belonging to St. Anne, the grandmother of Jesus, brought to France by Mary Magdalene, unaware that St. Anne is nothing more than a figment of the Catholic imagination.

The discovery of the remains, however, does nothing to alleviate the fears of the Church, for among the relics was missing one all-important piece. Although Jesus' body was discovered mostly intact, the records clearly maintain that the fragments were found "detached from the head," meaning that they were missing the skull.

The discovery of Jesus' remains in AD 792 marks the beginning of a five-hundred-year quest culminating in the unearthing of Mary Magdalene's sarcophagus in 1279. During this time, the whole of Europe, led by the Church, was gripped in the fever of finding this missing relic of Jesus, reverentially referred to as the "Holy Grail" - quite literally, the earthly cup that once housed the spirit of Jesus - his skull.

Sometime during the middle of the fifteenth century, a relic of extraordinary significance, supposedly belonging to Jesus' grandmother, St. Anne, arrives in Castelbuono - a small village on the island of Sicily that developed around its most prominent landmark,

Cappella Palatina, the "Palace Chapel" - Charlemagne's final resting place.

In this exquisitely ornate chapel, in an urn under a silver bust of Mary, symbolically still in the possession of a woman who poured every ounce of her being into its care, rests a skull with a missing jaw bone - every conceivable evidence suggesting that it belongs to that young preacher from Galilee who was betrayed twice: once when he was nailed to a cross, and again, when it was ensured that he stayed there.

The skull under the bust of Mary at Castelbuono, Sicily, Italy

About Avi

Born and raised in India, Avi's professional journey in the corporate world began soon after he graduated from college. However, at the age of 24, he recognized an emptiness within that material success could never satisfy. Yearning for inner tranquility and a sense of purpose, he made the courageous decision to move away from home, leave his job, and embark on a dedicated pursuit of meditation.

Devoting himself to intense meditation for three years, Avi underwent a profound spiritual awakening that forever transformed his life. Driven by this newfound realization, he eagerly began sharing his experience through various programs and retreats. In 2017, he traveled to America and intuitively knew that he had found a place to sow the seeds of consciousness and awareness.

Currently, Avi resides and teaches in Tennessee, where the first Nirvana meditation center is being developed. He speaks twice a day, and his talks are recorded and transcribed by his students, which are ultimately compiled into books for publication.

Nirvana Foundation is a nonprofit spiritual community providing individuals with an opportunity to explore the realms of meditation and self-awareness through books and programs.

Visit www.nirvana.foundation to learn more about Avi and his vision.

Further Reading

Armstrong, Karen, <u>The Battle for God</u>,
January 30, 2001, Ballantine Books

Armstrong, Karen, <u>The Bible</u>,
 November 1, 2008, Grove Press

Armstrong, Karen, <u>The Case for God</u>,
September 7, 2010, Anchor

Blech, Benjamin and Doliner, Roy,
<u>Sistine Secrets</u>, May 12, 2009, HarperOne

Borg, Marcus J., and Crossan, John Dominic,
<u>The Last Week</u>, January 30, 2007, HarperOne

Borg, Marcus J., and Kornfield, Jack,
<u>Jesus and Buddha</u>, January 12, 1999, Ulysses Press

Cahill, Thomas, <u>Desire of the Everlasting Hills</u>,
February 13, 2001, Anchor

Carroll, James, <u>Constantine's Sword</u>,
April 1, 2002, Mariner Books

Carroll, James, <u>Jerusalem, Jerusalem</u>,
April 4, 2012, Mariner Books

Crossan, John Dominic, <u>The Historical Jesus</u>,
February 26, 1993, HarperOne

Ehrman, Bart D., <u>The Lost Scriptures</u>,
September 15, 2005, Oxford University Press

Ehrman, Bart D., <u>Misquoting Jesus</u>,
February 5, 2007, HarperOne

Leloup, Jean-Lves, <u>The Gospel of Mary Magdalene</u>,
March 30, 2002, Inner Traditions

Mayotte, Ricky Alan, <u>The Complete Jesus</u>,
October 19, 2014, Create Space

Nicholl, Charles, <u>Leonardo da Vinci</u>,
November 18, 2004, Viking Adult

Robinson, James M., <u>The Nag Hammadi Library</u>,
November 21, 1990, HarperOne

Schaberg, Magdalene, <u>The Resurrection of Mary Magdalene</u>, June 7, 2002, Continuum

Shanks, Hershel, <u>Understanding the Dead Sea Scrolls</u>,
August 4, 1992, Random House

Spong, John Shelby, <u>Liberating the Gospels</u>,
November 25, 1997, HarperOne

Theissen, Gerd, <u>A Theory of Primitive Christian Religion</u>, October 1, 1999, SCM Press

Books by Avi

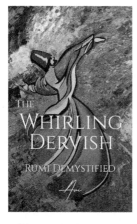

ISBN: 978-1962685009

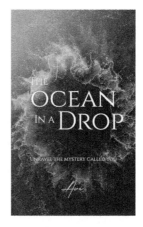

ISBN: 979-8852311207

ISBN: 979-8392250196

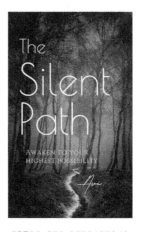

ISBN: 978-0578637068

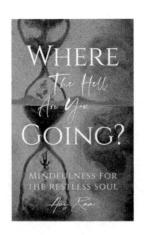

ISBN: 978-1962685023